Agricultural Policy and EU Competition Law

Agricultural Policy and EU Competition Law

Possibilities and Limits for Self-Regulation in the Dairy Sector

Dr. Anna Gerbrandy and dr. Sybe de Vries

Europa Institute Utrecht University

eleven
international publishing

Published, sold and distributed by Eleven International Publishing
P.O. Box 85576
2508 CG Den Haag
Tel.: +31 70 330 7033
Fax: +31 70-330 7030
e-mail: verkoop@budh.nl
www.elevenpub.com

Sold and distributed in USA and Canada
International Specialized Book Services
920 NE 58th Avenue, Suite 300
Portland, OR 97213-3786, USA
Tel: 1-800-944-6190 (toll-free)
Fax: +1 503 280-8832
orders@isbs.com
www.isbs.com

Printed on acid-free paper.

ISBN: 978-94-90947-11-8

Printed in The Netherlands

Table of Contents

1 Introduction

On 12 April 2010, Dacian Ciolos, Member of the European Commission Responsible for Agriculture and Rural Development, called for a public debate on the future of European common agricultural policy (CAP).[1] In his speech, the Commissioner focused on four strategic questions: [2]

- Why do we need a European Common Agricultural Policy?
- What are society's objectives for agriculture in all its diversity?
- Why should we reform the current CAP and how can we make it meet society's expectations?
- What tools do we need for tomorrow's CAP?

This is by no means the first time that the future of agricultural policy in Europe has been made the focus of discussion. In view of the complexity of European agricultural markets, however, this is hardly surprising.

With regard to the dairy market, upon which this contribution focuses, the European Commission's most recent plans for the future include limiting income support to dairy farmers, and abolishing milk quotas from 2015. However, as was also pointed out by Commissioner Ciolos in his speech, many questions regarding the future of the agricultural sector remain unanswered. Against the background of developments tending towards the abolition of certain intervention measures, it is interesting to consider whether any form of self-regulation by dairy farmers, with or without the support of the (national or European) government, might present an alternative for the regulation of the European dairy market. Such initiatives towards self-regulation may, however, be frustrated by the application of European and national competition rules.

This book focuses on the question of whether European agricultural legislation and competition rules offer any scope for self-regulation in the European dairy market. Within this larger question, certain sub-questions also arise: what are the relevant legal rules applicable to the dairy market, and what type of self-regulation is possible within the present legal framework?

---

1 Speech to the European Parliament's Agriculture Committee Brussels, delivered on 12 April 2010, SPEECH/10/150, available at: http://europa.eu/rapid/pressReleasesAction.do?reference=SPEECH/10/150&format=HTML&aged=0&language=EN&guiLanguage=en.

2 Ibid.

Chapter 2 contains a short summary of current European agricultural policy with regard to dairy farming, and indicates which parts of that policy are particularly likely to meet with opposition from the farmers concerned. Such opposition relates mainly to the abolition of milk quotas. As a result of the proposed abolition of milk quotas in 2015, dairy farmers fear that the market will become unstable, that the milk price level will become variable – potentially becoming insufficient for dairy farmers to maintain cost-effective production – and revenues generally will become insufficient to allow longer-term stability in dairy farming.

Chapter 3 addresses the question of whether the present rules of European law offer any scope for self-regulation by the dairy industry. The focus of this chapter is mainly on European competition law, and the relation between agricultural policy and competition policy. The conclusion is that there is some, though limited, scope for some form of self-regulation.

Chapter 4 deals with the question of whether the present rules can and should be amended in order to allow for the introduction of industry self-regulation. The conclusion, in short, is that either the exceptions within competition law will have to be stretched, or alternatively that necessary space will have to be created within agricultural policy.

Finally, chapter 5 contains a number of suggestions for modification of agricultural and competition policies in order to better serve the interests of dairy farmers.

2 European Agricultural Policy

2.1 Legal Basis and Framework

Treaty Provisions on Agriculture

From the beginning of European cooperation, the European CAP has occupied a prominent position in the European Treaties. The European Economic Communities (EEC) explicitly addressed the integration of agricultural activities. The explanation for this approach was that the agricultural markets in the member states used to be organized within the framework of market organisations, and because the application of the free movement provisions would undermine these market organisations, a common market in the sector could only be realized by means of the total communaliz ation of the national market organisation policies.[1] Agricultural policy is thus an instance of the most far-reaching form of integration: that is, a complete merger of negative and positive integration. The EEC Treaty, nor later Treaty texts, was not specific, however, regarding the exact measures to be taken as part of the implementation of this common policy.

Significantly, neither the EEC Treaty nor any relevant secondary regulations contain a clear definition of a 'farmer'. As a result, the decision as to who is to be regarded as a farmer is largely left to the member states, which in this matter enjoy a certain margin of discretion. This issue might play a role in the application of the exceptions in (TFEU or EU Functioning Treaty) (see section 4.3(c) below).[2]

Until recently, Articles 2 and 3 of the Treaty Establishing the European Community (EC Treaty), which contained the objectives and tasks of the European Community, served as the point of departure for the development of agricultural policy. However, the Treaty of Lisbon, which became effective on 1 December 2009, changed this legal framework. The EC Treaty was incorporated into the present EU Functioning Treaty, while the objectives of the European Union (EU) are now set out in the Treaty on the European Union (EU Treaty).

---

1 P. Kapteyn & P. VerLoren van Themaat, *Het recht van de Europese Unie en van de Europese Gemeenschappen*, 6th edn, Deventer: Kluwer 2003, p. 970.

2 See, e.g., J.A. McMahon, *EU Agricultural Law*, New York: Oxford University Press, 2007, p. 2-4. It is clear that 'milk' comes under the provisions relating to agriculture and agricultural policy, as Art. 38 TFEU states: 'Agricultural products means the products of the soil, of stockfarming and of fisheries and products of first-stage processing directly related to these products.'

The original Article 2 EC, which described the tasks of the EC, has largely been incorporated into Article 3 (3) of the EU Treaty, which now reads:

> The Union shall establish an internal market. It shall work for the sustainable development of Europe based on *balanced economic growth and price stability*, a highly competitive *social market economy*, aiming at full employment and social progress, and a *high level of protection and improvement of the quality of the environment*. The Union shall promote scientific and technological advance.
>
> ....
>
> The Union shall combat social exclusion and discrimination, and shall *promote social justice and protection* ....
>
> The Union shall promote *economic, social and territorial cohesion*, and solidarity among Member States. (Emphasis added.)

Article 3 (6) TFEU subsequently states that these objectives shall be pursued by appropriate means that are commensurate with the competences which are conferred upon the Union in the Treaties.

In Article 4 (2) TFEU, agricultural and fisheries policy is classified as a shared competence of the EU and the member states. According to Article 2 (2) TFEU, this means that the Union and the member states may each legislate and adopt legally binding acts. However, the member states shall exercise their competence to the extent that the Union has not exercised its competence. Such is the case in the field of agriculture, where the EU has frequently exercised its competence.

Agricultural policy is further based on the Title on Agriculture of the Treaty. Under Article 38 TFEU, the Union shall define and implement a common agriculture and fisheries policy. This provision, among other things, defines agricultural products (including milk and products of first-stage processing), but also – importantly for this contribution – defines the relationship between the internal market and agricultural policy, and shows that the internal market also extends to agriculture and that the internal market rules shall also apply to agricultural products.[3]

---

3 Art. 38, paras. 1, 2 and 4 TFEU provide:
The internal market shall extend to agriculture and trade in agricultural products.... Save as otherwise provided in Articles 39 to 44, the rules laid down for the establishment and functioning of the internal market shall apply to agricultural products.... The operation and development of the internal market for agricultural products must be accompanied by the establishment of a common agricultural policy.

Article 39 TFEU states the objectives of the CAP. It provides:

> 1. The objectives of the common agricultural policy shall be:
>   a. to increase agricultural productivity by promoting technical progress and by ensuring the rational development of agricultural production and the optimum utilisation of the factors of production, in particular labour;
>   b. thus to ensure a fair standard of living for the agricultural community, in particular by increasing the individual earnings of persons engaged in agriculture;
>   c. to stabilise markets;
>   d. to assure the availability of supplies;
>   e. to ensure that supplies reach consumers at reasonable prices.

The second paragraph of Article 39 indicates the special status of agriculture:

> 2. In working out the common agricultural policy and the special methods for its application, account shall be taken of:
>   a. the particular nature of agricultural activity, which results from the social structure of agriculture and from structural and natural disparities between the various agricultural regions;
>   b. the need to effect the appropriate adjustments by degrees;
>   c. the fact, that in the Member States agriculture constitutes a sector closely linked with the economy as a whole.

It should be noted that the Treaty of Lisbon has not altered these objectives. In order to attain the objectives of Article 39 TFEU, a CAP must be developed. Its form is prescribed in Article 40 (1) TFEU: it must contain 'a) common rules on competition; b) compulsory coordination of the various national market organisations; c) a European market organisation.' The second paragraph of Article 40 states:

> the common organisation (...) may include all measures required to attain the objectives set out in Article 39, in particular regulation of prices, aids for the production and marketing of the various products, storage and carryover arrangements and common machinery for stabilising imports or exports.

The relationship between competition law and agricultural policy is laid down in Article 42 TFEU (see further, section 4.1 below):

> The provisions of the Chapter relating to rules on competition shall apply to production of and trade in agricultural products only to the extent determined by the European Parliament and the Council within the framework of Article 43 (2) and in accordance with the procedure laid down therein, account being taken of the objectives set out in Article 39. The Council, on a proposal from the Commission, may authorise the granting of aid:
> a. for the protection of enterprises handicapped by structural or natural conditions;
> b. within the framework of economic development programmes.

The last two articles on agriculture relate to certain institutional provisions, which will not be dealt with in this contribution. It is remarkable, though, that Article 43 TFEU (finally) awards the European Parliament a right of co-decision in the field of agriculture.

These articles of the EU Treaty and the EU Functioning Treaty constitute the legal basis of the CAP, and indicate the possible scope for a deviation from the general rules on competition. They are also seen as an expression of the three components of agricultural policy:

a. the political-economic component, relating to the contribution of agriculture to economic growth;
b. the social-political component, including care for the rural population, including a stable income and rural development policy, which recently received a new impulse; and
c. the social-economic component, which relates to the food supply of consumers.[4]

The relative hierarchy of these elements, however, is not fixed: the European Commission sees to the coordination of the objectives, and may temporarily rank one above the other.

Another form for agricultural policy that is being discussed is based on 'two pillars': the first pillar comprises the common market organisation; and the second pillar comprises various forms of aid, but always related to specific investments, situations, services, or activities of the farmer.

Other Treaty Provisions relevant to the CAP and Competition Policy

In addition to the aforementioned provisions pertaining specifically to European agricultural policy, the EU Functioning Treaty contains provisions that are important to European

4 See, e.g., McMahon 2007, p. 21; see also, generally, J.S. Marsh & P.J. Swanney, *Agriculture and the European Community*, London: Allen & Unwin, 1980.

law and policy in general, and therefore also to agricultural and competition policy. Article 11 TFEU, for example, states that environmental protection requirements must be integrated into the definition and implementation of the Union policies and activities, in particular with a view to promoting sustainable development.

In addition, Article 13 TFEU reads as follows:

> In formulating and implementing the Union's agriculture, fisheries [...]policies, the Union and the Member States shall, since animals are sentient beings, pay full regard to the welfare requirements of animals, while respecting the legislative or administrative provisions and customs of the Member States relating in particular to religious rites, cultural traditions and regional heritage.

The integration provision of the Title on Culture, Article 167 (4) TFEU, may also be of importance. That provision states that the Union shall take cultural aspects into account in its action, in particular the diversity of its cultures.

Although the precise legal effects of these integration provisions are unclear, their importance should not be underestimated. Significantly, they are included in Title II of the EU Functioning Treaty under 'provisions having general application', and thus limit the discretionary power of EU institutions by requiring that environmental interests, animal welfare or cultural aspects are to be taken into account as part of agricultural or competition policy.[5] These aspects of common agricultural policy are thus strengthened. At the same time, the European Commission, the General Court, and the European Court of Justice will also have to take into account these interests in the implementation and enforcement of European competition rules. It should be noted that the European Commission, in case of major legislative initiatives, carries out impact assessments in which the social, economic and environmental effects of legislative proposals are assessed.[6] This aspect will be dealt with in more detail in section 4.3 below.

Finally, Article 14 TFEU on services of general economic interest may be important for determining the relationship between agricultural policy and competition law.

---

5 See also S.A. de Vries, *Tensions within the Internal Market – The Functioning of the Internal Market and the Development of Horizontal and Flanking Policies*, Groningen: Europa Law Publishing, 2006, p. 18-19.

6 For further information on these assessments, see http://ec.europa.eu/governance/impact/index_en.htm.

2.2 Developments

The CAP became very successful, but almost collapsed under that success: it resulted in overproduction. A reform process followed, which also applies in relation to the dairy sector. In 1984, quotas and levies were introduced.[7] This reform process, however, did not result in a reduction of the overproduction. As a result, the quotas were lowered.[8] The quota system triggered a multitude of lawsuits, but was in principle always approved of by the European Court of Justice as a legitimate measure by which to balance supply and demand. This interpretation is important, as it means that this regulatory system as such is not in violation of the Treaties.[9]

By 1991, a fundamental reform of the CAP was already under way: the relative relationship between the components mentioned above was restructured, and environmental protection grew in importance as part of general rural development policies. The reform resulted in the introduction of general measures compensating farmers for adopting environmentally friendly practices. For example, farmers were encouraged to set aside land for purposes other than agriculture. It is important to point out that the series of regulations in support of this new course aimed not only at encouraging environmentally friendly practices, but also at encouraging more diverse entrepreneurship, so that farmers would not remain exclusively dependent on agricultural activities for their income. In 2000, these reforms were assessed in Agenda 2000;[10] and they were considered to be successful, as they resulted in greater market balance and, on average, higher incomes. At the same time, however, the results for the environment appeared to be more mixed.[11]

Agenda 2000 also contained a programme for further reforms. Where agricultural policy had long been based on the provision of production aid – as a result of which farmers were encouraged to produce *more* – there was now a different form of encouragement, one which was output-driven. Farmers thus received direct income aid (instead of production aid), but demands were made regarding the means of production, the quality of production,

7 In Council Regulation 856/84, OJ 1984 L 90 of 31 March 1984, p. 10, which amended Council Regulation 804/68, OJ 1968 L 148/13 on the common organization of the market in milk and milk products.

8 Council Regulations 1355/86, OJ 1986 L 118 of 7 May 1986, p. 1 and 777/87, OJ 1987 L 78 of 20 March 1987, p. 10. The final system was laid down in Council Regulation 3950/92, OJ 1993 L 405 of 31 December 1992, p. 1.

9 See, e.g., Judgment of 13 December 1979, Case 44/79, *Liselotte Hauer v. Land Rheinland Pfalz*, [1979] ECR 3727 ; Judgment of 13 July 1989, Case 5/88, *Hubert Wachauf v. Bundesamt für Ernährung und Forstwirtschaft*, [1989] ECR 2609.

10 European Commission, *Agenda 2000 – A CAP for the future*, available at http://ec.europa.eu/agriculture/publi/review99/08_09_en.pdf.

11 McMahon 2007, p. 98.

and its management. Moreover, the phased abolition of quotas for milk was proposed. Agenda 2000also contained further developments of the rural policy: more attention was focused on the social aspects of the countryside, and also on the environment.

In the meantime, many of the measures proposed in Agenda 2000 have been introduced (some with modifications, others without), including the phased abolition of milk quotas (to be finally abolished in 2015). In 2002, the 'mid-term review' followed,[12] as a result of which (among other things) the single payment scheme (SPS) was introduced: aid in the form of an annual income allowance, linking the allowance to requirements regarding ecological policy (an approach referred to as 'cross-compliance'). The SPS payments will eventually, however, also be subjected to phased abolition. In 2007, the Commission launched the so-called 'health-check' of agricultural policy reform,[13] and repeated the health-check in 2009.[14] The health-check involves an assessment of the agricultural policy reform, and is designed to promote (even) more proposals for the simplification of rules (including, among other things, the general common market organisation) and the policy's effective implementation in member states.[15]

2.3 Special Characteristics of the Dairy Market

The proposed abolition of milk quotas has met with resistance, which is in particular due to the current historically low price of milk.[16] For example, Dutch dairy farmers, united in the Dutch Dairy Farmers Trade Union (NMV), are of the opinion that the abolition of all production regulations will endanger the stability of dairy supply, income levels for dairy farmers, and the conservation of the countryside. They consider fluctuations in the market price for milk in the past years as a sign of that instability. Within a one-year period, the price of milk reached both the highest (50 cents) and the lowest (20 cents) price level of the past thirty years.

---

12 Communication from the Commission to the Council and the European Parliament - Mid-Term Review of the Common Agricultural Policy, [COM (2002) 394, fin.], availabe at: http://eurlex.europa.eu/LexUriServ/LexUriServ.douri=CELEX:52002DC0394:EN:HTML

13 Communication from the Commission to the European Parliament and the Council - Preparing for the 'Health Check' of the CAP reform, [COM (2007) 722, fin.], availabe at: http://eurlex.europa.eu/LexUriServ/LexUriServ.douri=CELEX:52007DC0722:EN:HTML.

14 See http://ec.europa.eu/agriculture/healthcheck/index_en.htm.

15 The present common organisation is laid down in Council Regulation 1787/2003, OJ 2003 L 270/121 of 29 September 2003, amending Council Regulation 1255/1999, OJ 1999 L 160/48 of 17 May 1999 on the common organisation of the market in milk and milk products. This Regulation has been amended a few times. See for a summary of measures in force, see http://eur-lex.europa.eu/en/legis/latest/chap0360.htm.

16 Information on the protests of the Dutch dairy farmers, and the French and Spanish farmers, can be found at http://www.voorwie.eu/ec-en-handel/270-europese-commissie-blijft-bij-afschaffing-melkquota-melkveehouders-willen-juist-een-duurzaam-en-flexibel-quotasysteem.html.

There are a number of economic reasons that indicate why the market for milk is not a 'normal' market, in which milk production and price-setting are completely determined ruled by market mechanisms. The most important argument raised in this context is that it is impossible for an individual dairy farmer to regulate the market, in the sense that market-based incentives cannot be utilized. An individual dairy farmer cannot influence the total market production, and will therefore increase production in case of both a general production shortage and a general production surplus. In a shortage situation, with a high milk price, he will expand in order to increase his profit; and in a surplus situation, with a low milk price, he will expand in order to increase efficiency and to lower costs. Even in 2009, when the milk price was extremely low, the production of milk was stepped up: as a result, the surplus only increased, instead of the supply being adjusted to match the reduced demand.

Other arguments may also be presented in support of the statement that the market for milk is not a 'normal' market. The fact that milk constitutes basic food; the connection between milk production (at dairy farms) and the character of the countryside; and the importance of the countryside as a recreational, residential and living area for large parts of the population, bolster the view that the milk market is not a conventional market. In the Netherlands, though this may apply equally to other EU member states as well, the traditional Dutch cultural landscape containing the cow in the meadow has been under increasing pressure. In addition, dairy farmers may play an important role in the conservation of the natural environment.

The Commissioner for Agriculture has, however, indicated that he is not in favour of a quota reformulation for the time being. Instead, he regards other measures – some of which already exist – as solutions to the low incomes of dairy farmers. In June 2010, the High Level Group on Milk (High Level Group) presented seven recommendations for the EU dairy sector.[17] The High Level Group was established in 2009 as an initiative of the Commissioner for Agriculture – in the light of the impending expiration of milk quotas on 1 April 2015 – in order to discuss potential regulatory measures for the medium and long term, and to examine which measures might promote market stability, producers' incomes and market transparency. The Directorate-General of Competition of the European Commission also contributed to the report.

17 High Level Group, 'High Level Group makes 7 recommendations for EU dairy sector', Press Release IP/10/742, Brussels, 15 June 2010, available at http://europa.eu/rapid/pressReleasesAction.do?reference=IP/10/742.

The recommendations of the High Level Group address:

- contractual relationships between milk producers and dairies, where agreements in writing are entered into in advance of the delivery of raw milk, with provisions on price, quantity, time schedule and duration, possibly imposed by the member state;
- the collective bargaining position of the producers, in order to jointly negotiate with a dairy on their contractual conditions, including price;
- the role of interprofessional/interbranch organisations that might be comparable to the interprofessional/interbranch organisations in the fruit and vegetable sector;
- transparency in the dairy supply chain;
- market measures, marketing standards and origin labelling, and;
- innovation and research.

The European Commission intended to submit legislative proposals before the end of 2010 aimed at an improved structuring of the whole sector. Upon completion of this book, the Commission had indeed presented a proposal for a regulation,[18] aimed at boosting 'the position of the dairy producer in the dairy supply chain and prepare the sector for a more market oriented and sustainable future',[19] which in fact incorporates some of the findings presented in this book. However, the Commission again indicated that there are no reasons to 'revisit the Health Check decisions with regard to the gradual increase in quotas and the end of the quota regime on 1 April 2015',[20] leaving the planned phasing out of the quota-system intact.

Outside of Europe, properly functioning forms of self-regulation exist in dairy sectors. For the report of the High Level Group, four non-EU countries were asked to describe their market organisation and structure: the USA, Switzerland, Australia and New Zealand. These countries all acknowledge exceptions from the competition rules for dairy farmers, although the scope of these exceptions differs from country to country.[21]

Dutch dairy farmers, however, prefer to refer to the regulatory measures in force in Canada, which are based on the following principles:

18 Proposal for a Regulation of the European Parliament and of the Council, amending Council Regulation (EC) No 1234/2007 as regards contractual relations in the milk and milk products sector, [COM(2010) 728], to be found at http://ec.europa.eu/agriculture/milk/index_en.htm.

19 European Commission 'Commission proposes new measures to improve future stability in the dairy sector', Press Release IP/10/1691, Brussels, 09/12/2010, available at http://europa.eu/rapid/pressReleasesAction.do?reference=IP/10/1691.

20 European Commission at http://ec.europa.eu/agriculture/milk/index_en.htm.

21 See also High Level Group on Milk, *Report*, 15 June 2010, p. 11, available at http://ec.europa.eu/agriculture/markets/milk/hlg/report_150610_en.pdf.

- Canadian farmers have joined so-called 'pooling systems'. Six provinces concentrated in the 'Agreement on All Milk Pooling (P5)'. The remaining four provinces concentrated in the 'Western Milk Pooling Agreement'.
- These pooling systems enable dairy farmers to share their revenues, markets and some of their costs. One of the agreements even encompasses the sharing of all income by the farmers, so that everyone receives the same price for milk produced. By sharing markets, it becomes possible, in case of an increased demand in province A, for the farmers in other provinces to supply milk in order to meet this demand. Under this agreement, the dairy farmers share both the revenues and the costs for transport and promotion.
- It is the responsibility of the Canadian Dairy Commission to prevent overproduction by means of a national supply management system. On the basis of monthly information sent by provincial milk boards, the Canadian Dairy Commission calculates the quantity of milk each province is to produce in order to meet demand. This quantity is monitored during the year and, if necessary, amended. Apart from determining the milk price, the Canadian Dairy Commission also determines, on an annual basis, the prices for butter and skimmed milk powder.

In summary, the Canadian arrangement involves self-regulation by dairy farmers, but with government approval and oversight. It involves the assigning of quotas, in the sense of production regulation; and price setting, in the sense of imposed market prices for milk. A considerable investment was made in Canada to establish a system to regulate these aspects of the dairy market.[22]

European dairy farmers also wish to be able to regulate the dairy market *themselves*, in order to be able to produce in a market-oriented way and to earn their income through the maintenance of a cost-effective milk price. If this outcome were to be achieved, dairy farmers would no longer be (as) dependent on government aid and allowances, which could therefore be reduced or even abolished.

Self-regulation, however, must be embedded in a legal framework which is supported by government. In France, the first step was taken towards cooperation between dairy farmers and suppliers of dairy products when agreement was reached on an increase in milk prices. The French government intends to index the dairy sector, and to get actively involved in the market and price policy of the dairy sector in France. Within a national legal framework,

22 For information on the Canadian system, see, *inter alia*: http://www.voorwie.eu/nieuws/271-europese-commissie-houdt-vast-aan-afschaffing-melkquota-melkveehouders-willen-een-duurzaam-en-flexibel-quotasysteem.html.

vertical price agreements will be entered into, and the total number of producers permitted to participate in negotiations will rise from 400 to 4000. The French Minister of Agriculture has indicated a desire to promote this structural approach as far as possible within the framework of European competition law.[23] The question, of course, is whether the relevant European competition rules, which will be dealt with below, will permit such agreements.

23 For the report of the Committee on Economic Affairs in the French Senate, see *Compte Rendu Intégral du Senat*, Séance du Mardi, 27 April 2010, *Journal Officiel de la République Francaise*, n. 35 S. (C.R.) 2010, p. 2832.

3 Competition Law and Agricultural Policy after Lisbon

3.1 The Treaty of Lisbon and EU Policy on Competition

Since the entry into force of the Treaty of Lisbon, the concept of 'free competition' no longer features in the catalogue of objectives of the EU Treaty. Former Article 2 EU referred to the requirement to guarantee free competition as being an essential task necessary for the attainment of the objectives of the European Community. This task no longer appears in the current Article 3 EU. Instead, Protocol No.. 27 was attached to the Treaty, which states that 'the internal market as described in Article 3 [...] encompasses a regime which ensures that competition is not disturbed'.

The fact that competition is no longer mentioned explicitly as one of the objectives of the EU is attributed mainly to the French President Nicolas Sarkozy, who in doing so wished to stress – and probably simultaneously reassure his French constituency – that the EU does not exclusively advocate a pro-competitive and neoliberal market model. However, because a protocol possesses the same legal status as the Treaty itself, this raises the question of precisely what this alteration of the objectives might mean.

At the same time, however, the importance of a provision such as Article 3 EU, which lists the objectives and tasks of the EU, should not be underestimated. In various judgments, the European Court of Justice has referred to former Article 3 (1) (g) EU, and has drawn inspiration from this to support the fundamental character of the competition provisions.[1] However, the fact that free competition was not included in Article 3 EU, and that simultaneously a new concept, that of 'social market economy', was introduced in Article 3 EU, nevertheless indicates that social and other interests, such as the environment, might play a more prominent role in the ongoing process of market integration, and that such interests will also be taken into account in the application of competition provisions (see further section 4.3 below).[2]

---

1 See, e.g., Judgment of 21 September 1999, Case C-67/96, *Albany International BV v. Stichting Bedrijfspensioenfonds Textielindustrie*, [1999] ECR I-5751; see also Judgment of 20 September 2001, Case C-453/99, Courage, [2001] ECR I-6297.

2 See F. Amtenbrink & J. van de Gronden, 'Economisch Recht en het Verdrag van Lissabon I – Mededinging en Interne Markt', *SEW*, Vol 56, No. 9, 2008, p. 325.

3.2 The Prohibitions

In order to determine whether the EU rules on competition apply to the agricultural sector, it is important to determine whether these rules apply to farmers in general, and to dairy farmers in particular. The competition rules are stated to apply to 'undertakings'. According to the case law of the European Court of Justice, undertakings are entities that carry out an economic activity which consists of the offering of goods and services in the market.[3] This concept covers agricultural undertakings and dairy farms, including individual farmers: such producers offer their products in the market and exercise an economic activity, and are thus an undertaking within the meaning of the applicable competition law rules. The fact that a national company law, for example, does not recognize an undertaking as such, is irrelevant in this context.

The most important applicable competition rules are the *prohibition of cartels* and the *prohibition of abuseof a dominant position*. The latter prohibition is set out in Article 102 TFEU. The prohibition of abuse of a dominant positionentails that a dominant undertaking – that is, an undertaking (or group of undertakings) that controls over 40% of a market, and hence usually clearly occupies a dominant position in that market – must not abuse its position by engaging in certain types of prohibited conduct: for example, by imposing prices that are too low or too high, or by forcing competitors out of the market. For dairy farmers, this prohibition might be relevant in the context of the relationship between an individual (or a collective of) farmer(s) on the one hand, and supermarkets on the other; but for our present discussion it is of little relevance.

The prohibition of cartels is set out in Article 101 TFEU. In fact, the main rules of competition law are basically the same in both the Dutch and in the European context. The reason for this is that the Dutch Competition Act, which originally came into effect on 1 January 1998 (and which has subsequently been amended several times), is based on the EU rules.[4] In the following discussion, our focus will be mainly on the European rules on competition.

Article 101 TFEU prohibits:

> all agreements between undertakings, decisions by associations of undertakings and concerted practices which may affect trade between the Member States

3 Judgment of 23 April 1991 Case C-41/90, *Höfner and Elser v. Macrotron GmbH*, [1991] ECR I-01979.

4 For an unofficial English translation of this legislation, see Act of 22 May 1997, Providing New Rules for Economic Competition (Competition Act), available via the web site of the *Nederlandse Mededingingsautoriteit*, at http://www.nmanet.nl/engels/home/Legislation/10_Dutch_Competition_act/Index.asp.

> and which have as their object or effect the prevention, restriction, or distortion of competition within the internal market.

Specific interpretations of the concepts apply. The term 'agreement', for example, denotes a much broader set of arrangements than merely signed contracts. The concept of 'concerted practices' means that even if no agreement has yet been reached between undertakings, there may still be a prohibited coordination of behaviour: parties substitute practical cooperation for the risks of competition, thereby affecting the conditions of competition on the market.[5] The concept 'association of undertakings' comprises both formal and informal associations, and also includes interprofessional/interbranch organisations, such as, for example a federation in which dairy farmers are organised. A 'decision' by an association of undertakings is any action which results in some form of obligation being imposed on the relevant undertakings: a regulation issued by a national or coordinating European association of dairy farmers on production and prices would certainly fall within the scope of this prohibition.

The prohibition of cartels deals with agreements restricting *competition*. Article 101 TFEU itself provides a number of examples of such agreements: fixed prices (purchase price or selling price) are prohibited; and so are agreements on the assignment of quotas; agreements 'consisting of the limitation or control of production, markets, technical development or investments'; and agreements to share markets. To be caught by the provision, the agreement must restrict competition to an 'appreciable' degree. This means that if the impact on the market is only small – because the undertakings themselves are small, or because they only represent a limited market share – the prohibition does not apply. For the applicability of the European rules on competition, the notice on agreements of minor importance, or the *de minimis* notice, of the European Commission, is important. This issue will be addressed further below in section 4.2.

Finally, for the rules on competition to apply, trade between member states must be affected. In the classic *Grundig v. Consten* case, the European Court of Justice interpreted this condition as follows:

> What is particularly important is whether the agreement is capable of constituting a threat, either direct or indirect, actual or potential, to freedom of trade

5 Joined Cases 48, 49, and 51-57/69, *ICI v. Commission* (*Dyestuffs*), [1972] ECR 619, at para. 64.

between Member States in a manner which might harm the attainment of the objectives of a single market between states.[6]

Quotas and Levies

A regulatory approach that follows the Canadian example (discussed above in section 2.3), where a cooperation of farmers, or an umbrella organisation in which the farmers have united, agrees on quotas and fixes prices, in principle violates European prohibitions on competition-restricting agreements. In particular, price agreements in horizontal relationships and quota regulations are 'hard core' agreements that are almost always considered to fall within the scope of the prohibition of cartels.

It is important to point out that the prohibition of cartels relating to price agreements does not only relate to the 'whole' price of a product. Levies, allowances, or contributions representing only a (small) part of the price,[7] where the determination of the price is otherwise at the discretion of the undertakings themselves, nevertheless constitute a price agreement and are therefore in principle prohibited. Moreover, even in the case of 'voluntary' contributions, such as a voluntary contribution to a 'milk fund', it is likely that such contributions will also constitute a prohibited price agreement within the meaning of competition law, unless they are truly voluntary. This is not the case when, for example, contributions are coupled with voting rights relating to a federation's regulations, or when a recommendation from a federation's board is perceived by the the members as binding.

In addition, any levies imposed per unit of milk, where such levies are intended to regulate supply, may be regarded as constituting an indirect production restriction.

Although present competition law advocates the 'economic approach' to interpreting agreements, and focuses on the evaluation of an agreement in the economic and legal context in which it was conceived, price agreements and production restrictions still constitute the core of the prohibition. This is because the 'economic approach' is directed

6 Judgment of 13 July 1966, Joined Cases 56 and 58/64, *Établissements Consten S.à.R.L. and Grundig-Verkaufs-GmbH v. Commission of the European Economic Community*, [1966] ECR 299, at p. 341; see also the annotation by A. Gerbrandy in T.W.B. Beukers, H.J. van Harten & S. Prechal (eds.), *Het Recht van de Europese Unie in 50 Klassieke Arresten*, Den Haag: Boom Juridische uitgevers 2010, p. 30-31.

7 Besluit NMa, zaak 51, *Stibat*, 18 December 1998 en 31 May 1999". See also the VOTOB-decision of the European Commission (XXIInd Competition Report, 1992), which has been referred to as a missed opportunity for the Commission to integrate environmental considerations into its decision practice: F.O.W. Vogelaar, 'Towards an Improved Integration of EC Environmental Policy and EC Competition Policy: An Interim Report', in B.E. Hawk (ed.), *Annual Proceedings of the Fordham Corporate Law Institute – International Antitrust Law & Policy 1994*, The Hague: Kluwer Law International 1995, p. 554.

towards promoting consumer welfare , rather than market integration, as the primary objective of competition policy.[8]

In a way, this means that the evaluation of agreements is undertaken on a substantive rather than formal basis. Instead of the Commission or national competition authorities relying on an agreement's label when assessing its compliance with the competition rules, they consider instead its actual effect in the market. However, the economic approach offers little compliance flexibility should mutual agreements on quotas or (parts of) the price be considered : hard core agreements will hardly ever be permitted, even under the economic approach. The European Court of Justice in recent case law has confirmed this 'evaluation scheme'.[9]

Alternatives, such as Recommended Price and Information Flows

Where self-regulation by dairy farmers is concerned, the question arises as to whether alternative approaches can be found that restrict competition to a lesser extent. Proposals made by Dutch Dairy Farmers, aside from production restrictions by means of quotas and levies, relate to the adoption of recommended prices and the promotion of information gathering necessary for effective market analysis to be carried out by a Monitoring Institute. These two regulatory elements cannot be classified as 'hard core' restrictions. They may, however, have the *effect* of restricting competition. 'Effect restrictions' – that is, agreements that do not aim to restrict competition, but which nevertheless *may* have that effect as a result of their execution in the economic and legal context in which they are conceived – are also prohibited. An agreement establishing a recommended price may have such an effect, as through its performance it may practically function as a minimum price or a mutual price agreement. Although a recommended price may be intended to set the time to take action (that is, to intervene in the market), it may also fulfil an additional role for market participants. Whether this is in fact the case is a matter for investigation. [10]

---

8 See, for example, the literature on the Chicago School, especially R.H. Bork, *The Antitrust Paradox: A Policy at War with Itself*, New York: Basic Books 1978; and A. Jones & B. Sufrin, *EC Competition Law*, Oxford: Oxford University Press 2008, p. 28-30.

9 Judgment of 4 June 2009, Case C-8/08, *T-Mobile Netherlands BV and Others v. Raad van bestuur van de Nederlandse Mededingingsautoriteit*, [2009] ECR I-4529; see also the annotation by Gerbrandy in Beukers, van Harten & Prechal 2010, p. 34; see also A. Gerbrandy, 'Case Note, Case C-8/08, T-Mobile Netherlands BV, KPN Mobile NV, Orange Nederland NV, Vodafone Libertel NV v. Raad van bestuur van de Nederlandse Mededingingsautoriteit, Judgment of the Court (Third Chamber) of 4 June 2009', *Common Market Law Review* 2010-47, p. 1199-1220.

10 See, e.g., regarding vertical restraints, Jones & Sufrin 2008, p. 750.

In relation to the promotion of greater information flows, the sharing of market-sensitive information – especially the sharing of information on production quantities, on price setting or on new developments between undertakings that are each other's competitors – may also pose a problem for compliance with competition rules. This is particularly the case in oligopolistic markets, in which the mere *exchange* of information between competitors may weaken the market's competitive structure, even when this exchange takes place within or through an institute or industry body placed above the undertakings themselves. Although it is difficult for us to judge in the abstract whether information flows within a Monitoring Institute – or from a Monitoring Institute to dairy farmers – may be classified as a restriction, this potential risk should certainly be taken into account.

Coherence

As quotas and levies in principle clearly restrict competition, we will mainly focus on those two practices below. However, this does not alter the fact that other possible restrictions may play an important role. In addition, a regulatory approach comprised of a number of discrete parts, such as production restrictions and recommended prices, should also be viewed *as a whole,* as those parts support and possibly reinforce one another. The question of whether some form of self-regulation is nevertheless possible – despite the prohibition of cartels – due to the *objectives* such self-regulation pursues, is dealt with in more detail below in section 4.3.

3.3 EXCEPTIONS

European competition law contains a number of exceptions to the prohibition in Article 101 (1) TFEU. In seeking to invoke these exceptions, the analytical starting point should be that the competition law *does* apply – and that therefore, in principle, so too does the prohibition – but that competition law also provides scope for avoiding the prohibition of cartels contained in 101 TFEU. This analysis is, legally, different in nature from that which applies to the exception concerning the relationship between agricultural policy and competition law, in which competition law is considered simply not to be applicable at all (see below section 4).

Article 101 (3) TFEU

The first exception can be found in the third paragraph of Article 101 TFEU. This paragraph states:

> The provisions of paragraph 1 of this Article may, however, be declared inapplicable in the case of any agreement or category of agreements between undertakings, any decision or category of decisions by associations of undertakings and any concerted practice or category of concerted practices, which:
> *(1)* contributes to improving the production or distribution of goods or to promoting technical or economic progress,
> *(2)* while allowing consumers a fair share of the resulting benefit, and which does not:
> *(3)* a) impose on the undertakings concerned restrictions which are not indispensable to the attainment of these objectives; or
> *(4)* b) afford such undertakings the possibility of eliminating competition in respect of a substantial part of the products in question.
> (The numbers of the conditions shown in italics are added.)

If each of the four conditions set out in this exception is met, the prohibition shall not be applicable (and therefore the relevant agreement will be permitted). The Commission has elaborated these four conditions in a Notice.[11] This exception will be dealt with in further detail below (see section 4.3(b) below), in particular as part of the public interests that may be invoked to justify such an exception.

Article 106 (2) TFEU

Another exception that might be invoked is laid down in Article 106 (2) TFEU, and applies to undertakings entrusted with the operation of services of general economic interest. In order to invoke this exception, the following preconditions must be met:

- the relevant entrustment must be made by the government – to satisfy this requirement, action by a government is necessary (for example, by way of an administrative decision, an executive act, or the promulgation of a regulation);
- the undertaking must operate a service of general economic interest – these services are activities designated as such by the government, and may include the operation of public utilities, basic telephony services, basic postal services, and so forth; and

11 See Commission Notice of 24 April 2004 on the co-operation between the Commission and the courts of the EU Member States in the application of Articles 81 and 82 EC, OJ C 101, p. 97-118.

- an overarching proportionality requirement – the rules of competition law will only be inapplicable to the extent to which their imposition would prevent the undertaking from carrying out the relevant service of general economic interest.

This exception will also be discussed in greater detail below (see section 4.3(c)).

3.4 The Possibilities of Self-Regulation within the Prohibition of Cartels and the Available Exceptions

Above we have seen that even where the cartel prohibition is applicable, exceptions may be invoked. In the chapter 4 we will further explore these options (see sections 4.3(a) and (b) below). However, there are other possibilities for dairy farmers to balance their interests against the European competition rules. Chapter 4 shows that, despite the potential difficulties that may arise, there may also be possibilities for dairy farmers to avoid the prohibition of cartels altogether, when seeking to implement a strategy of self-regulation. The key relevant considerations are as follows:

- first, specific rules apply to the agricultural sector: some agreements fall completely outside the scope of competition law (see section 4.1 below);
- secondly, there also is the possibility of invoking the 'exception' for agreements that remain under a certain size: this relates to two tenets of competition law following naturally from each other: appreciability, and the *de minimis* rule (see section 4.2 below); and

A third possibility to explore is that it may be possible to take into account dairy farmers' interests *within* the scope of the prohibition (see section 4.3(a) below).

Additionally, as mentioned above, there are a number of true *exceptions.* Although exceptions by definition are interpreted strictly and there are only few precedents that could serve as a shining example, we will nevertheless discuss:

- the exception contained in Article 101 (3) TFEU (see section 4.3(b) below); and
- the exception for undertakings entrusted with the operation of services of general economic interest (see section 4.3(c) below).

4 The Relationship between Agricultural Policy and Competition Law

This chapter deals with the relationship between agricultural policy and competition law, and focuses on the following three questions:

1. Are the rules on competition applicable to the agricultural sector and, in particular, to the dairy sector?

If so:

2. To what extent does the requirement of appreciability offer scope for self-regulation to dairy farmers?
3. Alternatively, to what extent can the special character of agriculture and/or other objectives of general interest related to agricultural policy be taken into account in the application of the rules on competition?

4.1 The Relationship between Agricultural Policy and Competition Law

The starting point for our discussion is that the EU rules on competition are, in principle, applicable to all sectors of the economy. The provisions applicable to the relationship between agricultural policy and the internal market provisions, in particular the rules on free movement, are in general regarded as an integral part of the common market organisations.[1] Article 42 TFEU, however, states that the rules on competition shall only apply to the agricultural sector to the extent determined by the Council, which must take into account, among other things, the objectives set out in Article 39 TFEU (see section 2.1 above).

1 Opinion of AG Mengozzi of 16 September 2010, Case C-161/09, *Kakavetsos-Frangopoulos AE Epexergasias kai Emp SIA O.E. v. Nomarchiaki Aftodioikisi Korinthias* (*Kakavetsos-Fragkopoulos*), para. 34.

Council Regulation 1184/2006

To implement Article 42 TFEU, Council Regulation 26/62 was adopted; this was later replaced by Council Regulation 1184/2006.[2] Article 1 of the later Regulation provides that Articles 81 to 86 of the EU Treaty (now Articles 101 through 106 TFEU) shall apply to the production of, or trade in, the products listed in Annex I to the Treaty, including milk and dairy products. The applicability of those EU Treaty articles, however, is subject to Article 2 of the Regulation, which provides:

> Article 2
>
> 1. Article 81(1) of the Treaty (now: Article 101 (1) TFEU, *AG & SdV*) shall not apply to such of the agreements, decisions and practices referred to in Article 1 of this Regulation as form an integral part of a national market organisation or are necessary for attainment of the objectives set out in Article 33 of the Treaty (now: Article 39 TFEU, *AG & SdV*).
>   In particular, it shall not apply to agreements, decisions and practices of farmers, farmers' associations, or associations of such associations belonging to a single Member State which concern the production or sale of agricultural products or the use of joint facilities for the storage, treatment or processing of agricultural products, and under which there is no obligation to charge identical prices, unless the Commission finds that competition is thereby excluded or that the objectives of Article 33 of the Treaty (now: Article 39 TFEU, *AG & SdV*) are jeopardised.

Article 2 in fact contains *three* exceptions to the applicability of the competition rules. This may imply that farmers, including dairy farmers, have greater scope to implement regulatory measures that are in principle contrary to competition law. It should be noted that, on the basis of Regulation 1184/2006, it is *the Commission* which is exclusively entitled to determine whether Article 101 TFEU is applicable. National courts and national competition authorities may, however, apply Article 101 TFEU if they have ascertained that the agreements in question do not come under the exception of Article 2 of Regulation No. 1184/2006.[3] In addition, in the *Milk Marque* case, the European Court of Justice established that national competition authorities have both the power to review the objectives of

2 OJ L 214 of 4 August 2006, p. 7.

3 Judgment of 12 December 1995, Joined cases C-319/93, C-40/04 and C-224/94, *Dijkstra and Others v. Friesland (Frico Domo) Coöperatie and Others (Dijkstra)*, [1995] ECR I-4471. See also Court Rotterdam, 4 December 2001, MEDED 00/933-SIMO and MEDED 00/955-SIMO, *Stichting Saneringsfonds Varkensslachterijen (SSV) and U-Vlees B.V. v. DG of NMa*, para. 2.4.

Article 39 TFEU and the duty to reconcile these common agricultural policy objectives with competition law, analogous to the competence of the Community institutions.[4]

a First Exception of Article 2, Council Regulation No. 1184/2006

In the first place, an exception applies where agreements are entered into as part of a national market organisation and no common market organisation exists. This exception does not apply to the dairy sector, however, as a common market organisation does exist in respect of that sector. This exception, therefore, will not be considered further in this book.

b Second Exception of Article 2, Council Regulation No. 1184/2006

The second exception applies where the agreement is necessary for the attainment of the objectives set out in Article 39 TFEU. According to case law of the European Court of Justice, proof is required 'that the agreement is necessary for attainment of all of these objectives together'.[5] This means that the parties to an agreement must prove that the agreement is required in order to achieve all objectives of the common agricultural policy.[6]

In this respect, the *Meldoc* Decision, among others, is relevant.[7] In the *Meldoc* Decision, the European Commission concluded that the scope offered to corporations in the dairy sector by Council Regulation 804/68 for developing rules regarding a common market organisation for the dairy sector does not imply that those entities may agree upon price arrangements or lay down import restrictions. Such agreements would deviate too far from the intervention system imposed by that Regulation, and as a result the exceptions contained in Council Regulation 26/62 would not be applicable. As the intervention system in the dairy sector may undergo a radical change (as set out in chapter 2 above), which will probably *widen* the scope for private interventions, the question arises as to the impact of these provisions on the availability of the exceptions contained in Regulation 1184/2006. In the light of the *Meldoc* Decision, the fact that, at the EU level, milk quotas (for example) will be abolished, does not yet result in the introduction of such production restrictions through private initiatives. On the other hand, the *Meldoc* Decision was clearly related to import restrictions which have an adverse effect on the position of dairy businesses of

4 Judgment of 9 September 2003, Case C-137/00, *The Queen v. The Competition Commission, formerly The Monopolies and Mergers Commission, and Others, ex parte Milk Marque Ltd and National Farmers' Union*, [2003] ECR I-7975.

5 Judgment of 12 December 1995, Case C-399/93, *H.G. Oude Luttikhuis and others v. Verenigde Coöperatieve Melkindustrie Coberco BA*, [1995] ECR I-04515, para. 25.

6 Judgment of 15 May 1975, Case 71/74, *Nederlandse Vereniging voor de fruit- en groentenimporthandel, Nederlandse Bond van grossiers in zuidvruchten en ander geimporteerd fruit 'Frubo' v. Commission of the European Communities and Vereniging de Fruitunie (Frubo)*, [1975] ECR 00563, paras. 24-27.

7 Commission Decision 86/596/ of 10 December 1986, OJ L 348 (*Meldoc* Decision), p. 50-65.

other member states. When the European market is not split up, there seems to be more scope for private initiatives.

c Third exception of Article 2, Council Regulation 1184/2006

This is an exception that applies to practices taking place within a single member state which involve the production or sale of agricultural products, or the use of joint facilities for agricultural products. Until the Commission determines that the relevant cartelisation are detrimental to competition, or that the objectives of Article 39 TFEU are jeopardized, the validity of such practices cannot be challenged,unless they involve the obligation to charge a certain price.[8] This exception is most probably not applicable to the dairy sector, as the regulatory measures advocated by dairy farmers directly relate to price and production.

As a consequence, the scope for adopting measures within the framework of the applicable objectives is probably limited because of the existence of the common market organisation. Chapter 5, nevertheless, will address the possibility of exploring this scope, in consultation with the European Commission.

4.2 *The Appreciability Rule*

As previously mentioned, agreements that in principle restrict competition may nevertheless fall outside the restriction if they are not appreciable: that is, if they are not significant in the context of the market. Unlike the exceptions considered in sections 4.1 and 4.3, applying this rule does not involve striking a balance between possible 'public interests' and agricultural practices: it applies irrespective of any possible public interest-character of agriculture and agricultural products.

The appreciability rule has two manifestations: it is laid down in the *de minimis* notice of the Commission, but has a basis in case law of the European Court of Justice. In the *de minimis* notice, the Commission determines that, if undertakings that do not occupy more than 10% of the market are involved in horizontal agreements (that is, agreements between undertakings in the same phase of the production process, for example between the dairy farmers themselves, whether through an intermediate office or not), these agreements do not contravene the competition prohibitions.[9] However, this notice does *not* apply to 'hard

---

8 Joined cases C-319/93, C-40/04 and C-224/94, *Dijkstra*, [1995] ECR, I-4471, paras. 17-18.

9 Commission Notice of 22 December 2001 on agreements of minor importance which do not appreciably restrict competition under Article 81(1) of the Treaty establishing the European Community (*de minimis*), OJ C 368, p. 13-15.

core' agreements; and the scope of the benefit to be obtained under the notice thus remains limited for quota and price-setting arrangements. As a result, there is little scope for a mutual cooperation in that incorporates quota or price-setting even in limited forms as explained in section 3.2(a). Moreover, an effective self-regulatory structure in respect of the market would require much more than merely 10% of the market (that is, the farmers) to be participating. Further dividing the general regulatory structure into regional structures – even if that were practicable – would also be to no avail: those national structures would then simply be aggregated for the purposes of assessing the availability of the exception.[10]

The *de minimis* notice of the Commission is but an *elaboration* of the doctrine of appreciability as developed by the European Court of Justice,[11] intended to further legal certainty. Following the Court's doctrine, the appreciability requirement applies – in both EU and national law – regardless of the exact margins set by the Commission: if the impact of an agreement is negligible, the prohibition does not apply. The market-share margins in the *de minimis* notice, in a way, constitute a specific quantification of the threshold imposed by this doctrine. The appreciability doctrine of the European Court of Justice also has a qualitative aspect, although this is more controversial. We will discuss this aspect further below in relation to the proportionality test (see section 4.3).[12]

For dairy farmers making arrangements on quotas and prices, therefore, the chances of avoiding the prohibition of cartels on the basis of the appreciability exceptions are very limited. An interstate effect will easily be assumed, in view of the broad interpretation by the European Court of Justice of the fact that an agreement may impede trade between member states,[13] and the fact that mainly hard core agreements would be involved, which in any case fall under the prohibition of cartels.

4.3 *Taking into Account the Objectives of Agricultural Policy and the Dairy Sector within the Rules on Competition*

If the rules on competition are applicable to agricultural policy (and the dairy sector in particular), and the proposed self-regulatory approach is not so limited as to fall within

10 Judgment of 28 February 1991, Case C-234/89, *Stergios Delimitis v. Henninger Bräu AG*, [1991] ECR I-00935.

11 Judgment of 9 July 1969, Case 5/69, *Franz Völk v. S.P.R.L. Ets J. Vervaecke*, [1969] ECR 295.

12 In the Dutch Competitive Trading Act, a specific *de minimis* exemption to the prohibition of Article 7 (2) of that Act was created that does apply to hard core restrictions. Article 7 (2) of the Act provides that the prohibition does not apply – in case of horizontal agreements – if two cumulative requirements are met: first, the joint market share of the undertakings concerned *shall not exceed 5%* in the relevant market; and secondly, the joint turnover of the undertakings concerned *shall not exceed € 40,000,000*.

13 Since the judgment in Joined cases 56 and 58/64, *Grundig and Consten*, [1966] ECR 299.

the exception provided by the appreciability doctrine, it remains to be seen what scope the prohibition itself or the exception provides, taking into account the interests and objectives of the agricultural sector. As previously discussed in sections 2.1 and 3.1 above, the Treaty's legal context is relevant to agricultural and competition policy due to, among other things, the integration provisions regarding the environment and animal welfare.

The balancing of 'non-economic' or public interests against competition restrictions within the framework of EU competition policy has been a topic that has drawn considerable interest in recent years. Such a balancing consideration is also required on the basis of the integration provisions of the Treaty (see section 2.1 above).[14]

We will consider three possibilities in this context. For each, we begin with the details of the possibility in general, and then follow that summary by considering what this means specifically for dairy farmers.

4.3.1 *Article 101 (1) TFEU and the Doctrine of Inherent Restriction*

Inherent Restrictions and Interests of a Non-Economic Nature

If we observe the way in which the European Commission assesses agreements with regard to the prohibition of cartels, we find that in a number of cases so-called 'non-economic' interests, such as the protection of the environment, public health or culture, are taken into account. In view of the broad scope of the prohibition of cartels set out in Article 101 (1) TFEU, considerations of a non-economic nature can only be taken into account to a limited extent when applying Article 101 (1) TFEU. This applies in particular within the framework of the so-called 'inherent restriction' doctrine.

The inherent restriction doctrine relates to competition restrictions that are deemed necessary for the proper functioning of a market organisation or of a sector, and therefore do not fall under the prohibition of cartels of Article 101 (1) TFEU.[15] A good example of an inherent restriction is provided by the *Gøttrup-Klim* case,[16] which in fact concerns the agricultural sector. The case concerned provisions in the statutes of a cooperative purchasing

14 See generally, e.g., J.W. van de Gronden & K.J.M. Mortelmans, *Mededinging en Niet-Economische Belangen*, Deventer: Kluwer 2001; De Vries 2006; H. Vedder, *Competition Law and Environmental Protection in Europe; Towards Sustainability?*, Groningen: Europa Law Publishing 2003 and C. Townley, *Article 81 EC and Public Policy*, Oxford and Portland: Hart Publishing, 2009.

15 J. Houdijk, *Publieke Belangen in het Mededingingsrecht: Een Onderzoek in Vijf Domeinen*, Deventer: Kluwer 2009, p. 671.

16 Judgment of 15 December 1994, Case C-250/92, *Gøttrup-Klim e.a. Grovvareforeninger v. Dansk Landbrugs Grovvareselskab AmbA* (*Gottrup-Klim*), [1994] ECR I-05641.

association that prohibited the association's members from participating in other forms of organized cooperation that were operating in direct competition with the association. According to the European Court of Justice, such restrictions escape the prohibition in Article 101 (1) TFEU if 'they are restricted to what is necessary to ensure that the cooperative functions properly and maintains its contractual power in relation to producers'.[17]

In the *Wouters* case, the inherent restriction doctrine was applied to another sector, and further elaborated upon and extended.[18] The European Court of Justice held that deontological rules, such as (in the *Wouters* case) the prohibition introduced by the Netherlands Bar Association to prevent lawyers from entering into integrated cooperative arrangements with accountants, which was introduced in order to protect the bar's independence, constitute a justifiable exception to the prohibition of cartels. Whether *all* public interests will be able to profit from this approach seems to depend on the economic and legal context in which the decision was taken.

Another judgment of the European Court of Justice in the field of sport, the *Meca-Medina* case, shows that although an anti-doping regulation drafted by the Olympic Swimming Federation (and the sanctions resulting from a positive test finding) might entail competition restrictions, these provisions were restricted to what was necessary and proportionate to ensure legitimate objectives for the sector (here, the integrity of the competition, the preservation of the sportspersons' health, or to ensure the regular course of the games).[19] This approach applies a proportionality test to judge whether certain public interests are nevertheless justified in the light of the prohibition of cartels, despite the possible competition restrictions at stake. In fact, in both the *Meca-Medina* and the *Wouters* cases, the European Court of Justice directly balanced competition and public interests against one another in a manner that went beyond the strict requirements of the inherent restriction doctrine.[20]

The question that arises next is: what competition restrictions may be considered to be necessary and proportionate in the context of the prohibition of cartels? As mentioned previously, price arrangements, quotas and market-sharing agreements are often viewed as hard core restrictions, and are therefore not easily justifiable. However, if price constitutes

17 Case C-250/92, *Gottrup-Klim*, [1994] ECR I-05641, para. 35.

18 Judgment of 19 February 2002, Case C-309/99, *J.C.J. Wouters, J.W. Savelbergh and Price Waterhouse Belastingadviseurs BV v. Algemene Raad van de Nederlandse Orde van Advocaten, intervener: Raad van de Balies van de Europese Gemeenschap* (*Wouters*), [2002] ECR I-01577.

19 Judgment of 18 July 2006, Case C-519/04 P, *David Meca-Medina and Igor Majcen v. Commission of the European Communities and the Republic of Finland*, [2006] ECR I-06991.

20 See also Townley 2009, p. 132-133.

only one 'component' or one factor of a number of cost factors comprising a certain activity or service, an agreement might fall outside the scope of the prohibition of cartels. According to the European Court of Justice in the *Pavlov* case, the relevant agreement in that case did not restrict competition in an appreciable way.[21] This case dealt with the cost of a supplementary pension arrangement for medical specialists, not a field in which doctors compete with one another, and which only marginally influences the total cost of the services offered by medical specialists.[22] It is important to note that in the *Pavlov* case, the European Court of Justice took into account the fact that the price component represented by the cost of a supplementary pension arrangement for a medical specialist had little impact, in the end, upon the price to be paid in the market by the consumer of medical services.

Although the inherent restriction doctrine seems to provide greater freedom to serve public interests through private initiatives within the context of Article 191 (1) TFEU, prudence is called for.[23] The Court has not (yet) applied this doctrine to all sectors. It seems beyond doubt, however, that the specific characteristics of a certain sector are increasingly to be taken into account.[24] This is reinforced by the present central position of the integration provisions in the EU Functioning Treaty (see section 2.1 above).

Application to the Dairy Sector

To what extent can and must interests that are specifically related to the dairy sector be taken into account in the application of the rules on competition? It follows from the sections above that the agricultural sector is still regarded as a special sector, and that although competition rules are applicable to it, the objectives of agricultural policy must also be taken into account.

In applying the prohibition of cartels of Article 101 (1) TFEU, one could argue that the imposition of some measures restricting competition is necessary in order to realize objectives inherent to the agricultural sector. In view of the special character of this sector, and of the fact that its objectives are also explicitly included in the EU Functioning Treaty, agreements restricting competition need not automatically fall within the prohibition of cartels of Article 101 (1) TFEU. In the light of the *Meca-Medina* decision, this depends on the necessity and proportionality of the relevant agreements, and on the extent to which

21 Judgment of 12 September 2000, Joined cases C-180/98 to C-184/98, *Pavel Pavlov and Others v. Stichting Pensioenfonds Medische Specialisten (Pavlov)*, [2000] ECR I-06451 .

22 Joined cases C-180/98 to C-184/98, *Pavlov*, [2000] ECR I-06451, para. 95 .

23 Houdijk 2009, p. 97.

24 See also Judgment of 27 September 2006, Case T-168/01, *GlaxoSmithKline Services Unlimited v. Commission of the European Communities*, [2006] ECR II-02969 paras. 122-147.

such agreements are still justifiable in order to attain certain objectives, be they food supply, conservation of the natural environment or other public objectives related to agricultural policy. Further, in view of the broad approach of the Court in the *Wouters* and *Meca-Medina* cases, it is not inconceivable that such objectives will be balanced against the restriction of competition effected by the realization of the objectives.

In any case, the line is drawn where certain hard core restrictions of competition, such as the determination of quotas and prices, are included in agreements, unless, for example, the price is only a component of the total cost for the dairy farmers (consistent with the *Pavlov* case). With some effort, such an 'appreciability plea' could be made in favour of a levy for the benefit of establishing and maintaining a milk fund. If a levy (per unit of milk) is so minimal as to not, or to hardly, influence the price to be paid by the consumer, this reasoning might be valid. The difficulty lies in the criterion of the minimal influence on the price: there is just one example known in which the appreciability doctrine was applied in this way, and it will not easily be accepted that any price influence is minimal. Moreover, if the objective of imposing the levy is to finance a fund that, in times of excess supply, will pull the supply from the market (by means of an intervention), this may also be viewed as a production restriction. The proposed levy for the milk fund is only part of a broader system of proposed self-regulation; and while, unlike the *de minimis* margin, there is not an actual limitation of the size of the group that is allowed to participate in such a system of self-regulation, this aspect of qualitative appreciability, in the end, also provides at best an uncertain legal basis.

The discussion above demonstrates that the inherent restriction doctrine is still being developed: for the time being, it is unclear to what extent this doctrine will be followed by the competition authorities in the agriculture sector.

4.3.2 *The Exception of Article 101 (3) TFEU and 'Non-Economic' Interests*

As Article 101 (3) TFEU does not refer to public interests, to what extent can public interests be taken into account at all in the application of this provision? One interpretation of Article 101 (3) TFEU holds that it merely balances the competition restricting effects of a practice against the increase in economic effectiveness it produces.[25] Such an interpretation would limit the extent to which public interests such as environmental benefits, can be taken into account. Another interpretation however, considers that Article 101 (3) TFEU is founded upon a broader concept of welfare, and consequently also permits the

25 See, e.g., R. Whish, *Competition Law*, London: Butterworths, 2001, p. 125-128.

advantages of an agreement relating to consumer welfare to be taken into account.[26] In addition, reference can again be made to the integration provisions included in the Treaty that oblige the European institutions, when shaping and implementing policy, to take into consideration various public interests, such as Article 11 TFEU for environmental interests, Article 13 TFEU for animal welfare and possibly even Article 167 (4) TFEU for cultural aspects.[27]

There is indeed an increasing tendency to take public interests into consideration, a tendency which is most visible in the area of the environment.[28] The CECED order of the European Commission[29] shows that the positive effects of an agreement for society as a whole, and not only for individual consumers, may fall within the scope of Article 101 (3) TFEU. In respect of agreements restricting competition that are aimed at the realization of environmental objectives, the Commission did regard environmental advantages as constituting direct advantages for the consumer.[30]

In applying the proportionality test, the consumer's interest is often not regarded as a separate and distinct interest, but is rather included as part of the broader positive economic effects of the relevant cooperation. Moreover, environmental cases show that cost reduction for consumers is not always regarded as a necessary part of the proportionality test: improvement of the quality of the environment may also be regarded as being positive for consumers, even if this leads to price increases in the short term. The proportionality principle is of major importance, as the justifiability of agreements or practices restricting competition is ultimately judged on the basis of this principle.

Two other relevant examples of the application of the conditions of Article 101 (3) TFEU are the *Ford/Volkswagen* Decision[31] and the *Stichting Baksteen* Decision[32] by the Commission. (It is important to note, however, that these decisions are somewhat older, and their relevance for the present should therefore be assessed with some caution.) In the former decision, the Commission took into consideration the creation of jobs and the attraction of investors in determining that the conditions of Article 101 (3) had been fulfilled.[33] This

26 G. Monti, 'Article 81 EC and Public Policy', *Common Market Law Review*, 39, 5, 2002, p. 1065.
27 See also, generally, De Vries 2006.
28 See generally, e.g., Vedder 2003.
29 Commission Decision 2000/475 (CECED), OJ 2000 L 187/47.
30 Ibid; see also Commission Decision 94/332, (*Exxon/Shell*), OJ 1994 L 144/20.
31 Commission Decision 93/49 (*Ford/Volkswagen*), OJ 1993 L 20/14.
32 Commission Decision 94/601 (*Stichting Baksteen*), OJ 1994 L 131/15.
33 It should be noted that this decision was also made under the old system, whereby Article 81 (3) EC (now Article 101 (3) TFEU) did not have a direct effect (as is now the case), and one still had to request an

concerned the establishment of a car factory in one of the (at the time) poorest parts of Europe, namely Portugal, as a result of which 5,000 jobs would be created directly, and possibly another 10,000 more jobs indirectly. In addition, the establishment of this car factory would attract other investments. All other requirements of Article 101 (3) TFEU were (also) met, but this consideration did play a role in the evaluation.

In the *Stichting Baksteen* Decision, the Commission decided that the requirements of Article 101 (3) TFEU had been met, despite the fact that the agreement between the brick producers contained a production restriction. A production restriction is normally deemed to be a very serious issue in the competition context. This production restriction, however, had been agreed upon as part of restructuring measures aimed at – permanently – eliminating overcapacity from the market. The Commission took into consideration the fact that, as a result of these agreements, the restructuring process would take place under socially acceptable conditions (phased reductions, orderly conduct), instead of through much more disruptive sudden bankruptcies.[34]

Nevertheless, the European Commission's policy in the field of public interests and competition policy has not yet fully crystallized. Marginal 42 of the guidelines on the application of Article 81 (3) EU (now Article 101 (3) TFEU) shows that the Commission adopts a more cautious approach in assessing other public interests with regard to Article 101 (3): 'Objectives pursued under other Treaty provisions may be taken into account to the extent that they can be classified under the four conditions of Article 101 (3).'[35]

Application to the Dairy Sector

Article 101 (3) EU seems to offer scope for the pursuit of public interests by undertakings, including by Dutch (and European) dairy farmers. In the sections above, the conclusion was drawn that, in the context of Article 101 (3) TFEU, environmental advantages can be taken into consideration, including advantages which are only long-term and which benefit society as a whole rather than individual consumers. This is important for dairy farmers, particularly given the role of dairy farmers' in conservation of the natural environment, landscape development and the improvement of the environment. Consideration might also be given to the principle that usually products produced close to home have lower environmental impact – often expressed as a 'lower environmental or ecological footprint' – than products that are literally 'far-fetched' from remote production zones. It

exemption. For this reason, the Commission has commented on this procedure in a decision: see Commission Decision 93/49 (*Ford/Volkswagen*), OJ 1993 L 20/14.

34 Commission Decision 94/601 (*Stichting Baksteen*), OJ 1994 L 131/15. See also Commission Decision 84/380 of 4 July 1984 (*Synthetische Vezels*), OJ 1984 L 207/17.

35 Notice Commission application Article 81 (3) of 27 April 2004, OJ C 101 , p. 97-118.

is, however, difficult for us to assess the actual validity of this reasoning, given the underlying complexities in comparing and assessing production methods and the cost of transportation. Food safety issues may also play a role. Therefore, if dairy farmers enter into agreements that clearly contribute to the attainment of these positive objectives, it is in principle possible to invoke Article 101 (3) TFEU.

If the aims of self-regulation also include the prevention of socially unacceptable conditions in the market and the reduction of overcapacity – which might be necessary due to the specific competition characteristics of the milk market – and moreover if self-regulation seeks to contribute to sustainable long-term conditions of dairy farming, the argument based on Article 101 (3) TFEU is strengthened. However, although environmental objectives have increasingly become accepted, the more 'social' aspects of restrictive regulations still pose a somewhat open-ended question.

The European Court of Justice has decided previously that a long-term objective may be essential when an appropriate justifying basis is invoked. In the *Romkes* and *Kramer* cases, the Court held that restrictive national fishing measures are not measures having the same effect as quantitative import restrictions within the meaning of Article 34 TFEU (free movement of goods), due to the fact that these measures, although leading to a reduction of the quantities of fish that can be traded between the member states in the short term, are designed to ensure optimal returns for the fishing industry in the long term.[36] It should be noted, though, that in *Romkes* and *Kramer* it was *government measures* that were assessed with regard to – among other things – Article 34 TFEU, which offers more scope than does Article 101 TFEU for the justification of production restrictions. Public interests are, in the first place, guaranteed by the government.[37]

Public interests are taken into account, to a greater or lesser extent, not only in the environmental field, but also in other fields such as health care and culture. Unlike the inherent restriction doctrine, all four conditions of Article 101 (3) TFEU must, however, be met before dairy farmers can successfully invoke the exemption it provides. This may pose a problem, as the instrument of self-regulation envisaged by the dairy farmers must be necessary for attainment of the objectives and may not go any further than necessary to achieve that purpose. Much then depends on the exact formulation of the approach to regulation that is adopted, and the objectives that one (actually!) tries to realize by using it.

36 Judgment of 16 June 1987, Case 46/86, *Albert Romkes v. Officier van Justitie for the District of Zwolle* (*Romkes*), [1987] ECR 02671 para. 24; and Judgment of 14 July 1976, Joined cases 3, 4 and 6/76, *Cornelis Kramer and others (Biological resources of the sea)* (*Kramer*), [1976] ECR 01279.

37 De Vries 2006, p. 337.

4.3.3 *Services of General Economic Interest under Article 106 (2) TFEU*

Undertakings Entrusted with Services of a General Economic Interest

Article 106 (2) TFEU contains an explicit exception for undertakings entrusted with the operation of services of a general economic nature. This provision is not only relevant for Article 106 (1) TFEU, but also for other provisions of the EU Functioning Treaty, such as, for example, the prohibition of state aid or the prohibition of cartels. In order to invoke Article 106 (2) TFEU, the relevant undertaking must be entrusted with a task of general economic interest, and this task must be clearly described in national legislation. The point of departure for the definition of, and entrustment with, tasks of general economic interest is, according to established case law, that the member states possess wide discretionary powers, and that the Commission only tests the definition for manifest errors.[38] This broad power of the member states may (partly) be explained by a number of factors, including: that the EU Treaty and the EU Functioning Treaty each lack a definition of 'services of general economic interest'; that Article 14 TFEU stresses the importance of such services; and that in a number of fields – such as health care and house construction – the member states are primarily competent to take measures. However, in other fields, such as the environment, where the member states and the Community have a shared competence, the member states also possess wide discretionary powers to define services of general economic interest and to entrust the performance of such services to appropriate undertakings.

Application to the Dairy Farmers

This last possibility to escape the prohibition of cartels is only important to undertakings that have been entrusted with the task of performing a service of a general economic interest *by the member state*. If dairy farmers are increasingly confronted with tasks and obligations regarding nature and the environment, such as nature conservation and landscape management, they should request that the government entrust them with responsibility for these tasks in an explicit way, that is by means of regulations or legislation. Those undertakings can then invoke Article 106 (2) TFEU and obtain all the advantages deriving from those provisions.

The proportionality test, as briefly discussed above, is in this context carried out in a 'milder' way than in the framework of Article 101 (3) TFEU. But dairy farmers will still have to negotiate with their own national governments in order to be entrusted with relevant tasks.

---

38 Judgment of 12 February 2008, Case T-289/03, *British United Provident Association Ltd (BUPA) and Others v. The Commission of the European Communities and Others* (*BUPA*), [2008] ECR II-00081.

The problem with this approach, when considered in the light of potential or proposed self-regulatory approaches, is that hard core restrictions will rarely meet the proportionality test.

5 Possibilities of Adjusting Agricultural and Competition Policy

The preceding discussion shows that, although there is some scope for self-regulation within the context of the rules on competition, this scope is still very limited. In this chapter, we will therefore explore the possibilities available within European law for creating legal instruments that better safeguard the interests of dairy farmers in the Netherlands and in Europe.

5.1 Agricultural Policy

Although agricultural policy is a shared competency of the EU and the member states, on the basis of the EU Treaty, in practice the European legislator has often claimed this competence. As a result, member states generally only carry out such tasks in 'joint administration' with the EU. For dairy farmers, this means that they must seek to influence EU policy, even if only through national channels, with a view to, for example, the abolition of the phasing out of the quota system. (National advocacy is required, despite the claimed competence by the European legislator, because agricultural policy is largely prepared on a national level.) However, in the light of the current plans of the European Commission referred to above, this is not a realistic option.

Another option is the establishment of a European framework in which self-regulation as envisaged by dairy farmers is embedded. The conditions of an interventional system based on the Canadian example are already being formulated at the EU level. Adopting such an approach would mean that self-regulation by dairy farmers would acquire a clear legal basis. The present political climate seems to offer the momentum to advocate such a framework. In the Summary of Recommendations contained in its report of 15 June 2010, the High Level Group on Milk, for example, considers that:

> 'there is a need to increase awareness and reinforce the responsibility of the operators in the dairy chain to better take into account the signals of the market and adapt supply to demand. Therefore the HLG invites the Commission to consider the most appropriate manner, whether by guidelines or a legislative

> proposal, to enhance on a voluntary basis the use of formal written contracts, made in advance, to cover deliveries of raw milk…'

The essential elements of such an agreement would be price and supply volumes.

In the Council meeting on agriculture and fisheries held on 27 September 2010, a large majority of member states (22) appeared to support the conclusions of the High Level Group, and appealed to the Commission to respond, in particular to the following three recommendations of this Group:

- the setting of better contractual conditions between milk producers and dairy factories;
- increasing the collective bargaining power of the producers; and
- investigating the possible role of interprofessional/interbranch organisations in the dairy sector.

Upon finishing the text of this book the Commission has indeed resented a proposal in reaction to the recommendations of the High Level Group. In this regard, it is also important that, since the Treaty of Lisbon, the European Parliament has gained an active role in the decision-making process (see also section 2.1 above), and may therefore also be called upon to further the interests of dairy farmers.[1]

5.2 *Agricultural Policy and Competition Law*

Not only agricultural policy as a whole, but also the application of the second exception of Article 2 of Regulation 1184/2006, may offer a solution for dairy farmers. As previously mentioned, this Regulation pertains to the need to attain the objectives of Article 39 TFEU. From the viewpoint of dairy farmers, the issue is that an agreement would be necessary for attainment of all the objectives of the common agricultural policy. Agricultural policy consists of three components:

- the political-economic component, where agriculture contributes to economic growth;
- the social-political component, including care for the rural population, providing a stable income, and rural policy ('rural development'), that more recently has received a new impulse; and
- the social-economic component, that concerns the food supply of consumers, (see section 2.1 above).

1 See also the Press Release of 26 October 2010, 15357/10 (provisional version) of the 3042nd Council Meeting, available at http://www.consilium.europa.eu/uedocs/cms_data/docs/pressdata/en/agricult/117419.pdf.

The issue at hand is not merely related to providing a stable income. The proposed self-regulatory approach is intended to actually contribute to rural development – the arguments for this follow naturally from those supporting stable incomes, but also go beyond that – and the maintenance of a safe food supply. For that purpose, one might consider quality requirements. These quality requirements, however, may in their turn not necessarily restrict competition.

The recommendations of the High Level Group also relate to quality standards and innovation in common agricultural policy, in particular in relation to rural development policy. The dairy sector is therefore also invited to think about the competitiveness of the food chain generally.

5.3 *Guidance from the European Commission within the Framework of Competition Law?*

The European Commission has the power to assess agreements or regulations that are of major interest *ex ante*: for example, agreements or regulations which present a novel legal question. In order to prevent the reforms introduced by Council Regulation 1/2003 from being undone by over-generously awarded opportunities to seek this 'informal' guidance from the Commission, the Commission has drafted more detailed conditions for requisting such guidance in a Notice.[2] Point 8 of the Notice reads as follows:

> Subject to point 7, the Commission, seized of a request for a guidance letter, will consider whether it is appropriate to process it. Issuing a guidance letter may only be considered if the following cumulative conditions are fulfilled:
>
> a. The substantive assessment of an agreement or practice with regard to Articles 81 and/or 82 of the Treaty, poses a question of application of the law for which there is no clarification in the existing EC legal framework including the case law of the Community Courts, nor publicly available general guidances or precedent in decision-making practice or previous guidance letters.
> b. A prima facie evaluation of the specificities and background of the case suggests that the clarification of the novel question through a guidance letter is useful, taking into account the following elements:
>   - the economic importance from the point of view of the consumer of the goods or services concerned by the agreement or practice, and/or

2 Commission Notice on informal guidance relating to novel questions concerning Articles 81 and 82 of the EC Treaty that arise in individual cases (guidance letters), OJ 2004 C 101/78.

- the extent to which the agreement or practice corresponds or is liable to correspond to more widely spread economic usage in the marketplace, and/or
- the extent of the investments linked to the transaction in relation to the size of the companies concerned and the extent to which the transaction relates to a structural operation such as the creation of a non-full function joint venture.

c. It is possible to issue a guidance letter on the basis of the information provided, i.e. no further fact-finding is required.

The proposed legal question can be submitted to the Directorate-General for Competition, accompanied by a detailed plan, as to whether a regulatory measures envisaged by the dairy farmers might be accepted under the 'inherent restriction doctrine', whether that regulation might – under the *Pavlov* formula – escape the prohibition, or whether it might fall under the exemption of Article 101 (3) TFEU. The framework of competition law as discussed previously shows that the scope of such exceptions is limited: the relevant regulatory measure would have to focus as little as possible on actual interventions in prices and production, and as much as possible on the interests served by agriculture and the dairy sector as a whole. A price regulation, therefore, is a sensitive issue; so too is a buy-up scheme which seeks to mitigate situations of overproduction.

Moreover, a regulatory measure would be especially of use if it applies Europe-wide. A measure that focuses only on an individual member state, such as the Netherlands or France, may be useful from a national perspective, but may also result in national farmer groups pricing themselves out of the European market: for example, if they were the only participants within that market to impose a levy on their milk price. This view is important, as even in case of a national regulatory scheme, European rules on competition will (also) be applicable: a regulatory measure that covers the majority of dairy farmers in the Netherlands will also have an effect on interstate trade. Moreover, press releases show that the underlying reason for price arrangements between dairy farmers and suppliers of dairy products in France is generally income preservation for the French dairy sector in times of tough competition from the German dairy sector. This lends the call for a European approach even greater urgency.

The High Level Group has proposed arrangements between dairy farmers and dairy producers – vertical arrangements – on prices and quantity in order to better respond to market signals, and to match supply with demand. This also seems to be the goal of the French relevant regulations.

From the perspective of competition law, the creation of a fund drawn from imposing a small levy on the milk production could be an alternative structure. The creation of such a fund would involve a certain amount of price-setting, which in a general sense is a sensitive issue in competition law. However, if the fund restricts itself to setting only a marginal part of the price, as a result of which the effect on the consumer's price is nil, it could be argued that its influence on competition is not appreciable (via the *Pavlov* interpretation). Regarding the establishment of a fund and production restrictions in general, it is important to substantiate precisely what goals are being pursued by such regulatory approaches. The central interests served by a fund and quotas are the prevention of overproduction and the stabilization of the market, which – in the long term – seek to achieve a number of valid goals, including the conservation of the countryside, ecological management, and the maintenance of a good quality food supply. How then does the regulatory approach as advocated by dairy farmers contribute to these goals of general interest? It needs to be emphasized that the more prominently the relevant general interest – protection of the environment (through facilitating supply source close to home), ecological management, the conservation of the natural environment, food supply, and quality standards, for example – *actually* features in the dairy farmers' perception of themselves, the more scope competition law will offer for such a self-regulatory approach. The Commission has many years of experience with competition law, and quickly and easily sees through a price arrangement coated with a thin layer of veneer.

It is also important for dairy farmers to substantiate why such self-regulation is necessary *over and above* the existing regulations of agricultural policy: where do these existing measures fail to provide dairy farmers with adequate support?

5.4 *Lobby for an Entrusted Task of General Economic Interest*

As explained above, dairy farmers might – with the emphasis on *might* – seek to invoke the exception as laid down in Article 106 (2) TFEU for undertakings entrusted with a service of general economic interest. However, this is only possible if the national government – acting, for example, through the Ministry of Economic Affairs and Agriculture – expresses its view by way of a regulation, a ministerial decision or in any other unambiguous way, on the role of the dairy sector as a whole in, for example, the conservation of the natural environment, ecological management, the supply of basic food, and so forth.

Furthermore, the Treaty of Lisbon provides the European legislator with the option to issue a regulation on the basis of Article 14 TFEU for services of a general economic nature, which might also include the dairy sector.

Such a national or European regulation is, however, not to be expected on short notice. Further, even if a minister expresses his views to this effect, the scope of this strategy for dairy farmers is not unlimited: the rules on competition remain valid unless the application thereof *prevents* the performance of the entrusted task.

6 Conclusion

We conclude that, although European rules present opportunities for self-regulation to dairy farmers, these are as yet quite limited. EU competition rules – and possibly national competition legislation – constitute the general framework for a review of any proposed self-regulation initiatives, unless the exception within Article 2 of Regulation 1184/2006 applies. However, this exception has been interpreted very strictly by the European Court of Justice and the European Commission.

In view of the competition rules, it is important to fashion self-regulation in such a way that no 'hard core' restrictions on competition are imposed. Agreements on price and production are in principle likely to be objectionable, unless, for instance, the price is only a small component of a broader set of arrangements between dairy farmers. At the same time, developments in competition law show that the specific characteristics of a sector, such as the agricultural sector, and public interests, such as the protection of the environment, conservation of the natural environment and the development of the countryside, will increasingly be taken into consideration. The Treaty of Lisbon strengthens the social (and public) dimension of the internal market, as a result of which 'non-economic interests' are to be taken into consideration more than was previously the case in the application of competition law.

In order to ensure that initiatives for self-regulation are not ultimately frustrated by the application of competition rules, it is essential to exert influence on politicians and competition authorities at the European and at the national level. Dairy farmers can take action and develop strategies in support of their plans for self-regulation on various fronts. The very establishment of a High Level Group shows that the Council is not insusceptible to the application of appropriate pressure and lobbying. On the basis of the results of the investigation by the High Level Group, the Commission has now been requested at a high level to present legislative initiatives in relation to dairy-sector self-regulation. European legislation, then, may form the legal framework that provides scope for further arrangements between dairy farmers and dairy producers, and may help to mitigate the effects of the application of competition rules to the dairy sector.

Bibliography

Ambtenbrink & Van de Gronden 2008
F. Amtenbrink en J. van de Gronden, 'Economisch Recht en het Verdrag van Lissabon I - mededinging en interne markt', *SEW*, 2008, p. 325.

Bork 2008
R.H. Bork, *The Antitrust Paradox: A Policy at War with Itself*, Basic Books, 1978

Gerbrandy 2010
A. Gerbrandy, 'Case Note Case C-8/08, T-Mobile Netherlands BV, KPN Mobile NV, Orange Nederland NV, Vodafone, Libertel NV v. Raad van Bestuur van de Nederlandse Mededingingsautoriteit, Judgement of the Court (Third Chamber) of 4 June 2009, *CML Rev.*, 2010-47, p. 1199-1220.

Gerbrandy
A. Gerbrandy, 'Consten en Grundig', in: *Het Recht van de Europese Unie in 50 klassieke arresten,* Den Haag: Boom Juridische Uitgevers 2010, p. 29-37.

Van de Gronden & Mortelmans 2001
J.W. van de Gronden en K.J.M. Mortelmans, *Mededinging en niet-economische belangen*, Deventer: Kluwer 2001.

Jones & Sufrin 2008
A. Jones & B. Sufrin, *EC Competition Law*, Oxford: Oxford University Press, 2008, p. 28-30.

Houdijk 2009
J. Houdijk, *Publieke belangen in het mededingingsrecht: een onderzoek in vijf domeinen*, Deventer: Kluwer 2009.

Kapteyn & VerLoren van Themaat 2003
Kapteyn & VerLoren van Themaat, *Het recht van de Europese Unie en van de Europese Gemeenschappen*, Deventer: Kluwer 2003.

Marsh & Swanney 1980
J.S. Marsh & P.J. Swanney, *Agriculture and the European Community*, Londen: Allen and Unwin 1980.

McMahon 2007
J.A. McMahon, *EU Agricultural Law*, New York: Oxford University Press 2007.

Monti 2002
G. Monti, 'Article 81 EC and public policy', *Common Market Law Review* 2002.

Townley 2009
C. Townley, *Article 81 EC and public policy*, Oxford and Portland: Hart Publishing 2009.

Vedder 2003
H. Vedder, *Competition Law and Environmental Protection in Europa; Towards Sustainability?*, Groningen: Europa Law Publishing 2003.

Vogelaar 1994
F.O.W. Vogelaar, 'Towards an Improved Integration of EC Environmental Policy and EC Competition Policy: An Interim Report', in: B.E. Hawk (Ed.), *Annual Proceedings of the Fordham Corporate Law Institute – International Antitrust Law & Policy* 1994, The Hague: Kluwer Law International 1995.

De Vries 2006
S.A. de Vries, *Tensions within the Internal Market – The Functioning of the Internal Market and The Development of Horizontal and Flanking Policies*, Groningen: Europa Law Publishing 2006.

Whish 2001
R. Whish, *Competition Law*, London: Butterworths 2001.

Index

Table of Cases

European Court of Justice

General Court

Court Rotterdam

Table of Articles

Landbouwbeleid en EU-mededingingsrecht

Landbouwbeleid en EU-mededingingsrecht

Mogelijkheden en grenzen voor zelfregulering in de melksector

Dr. mr. Anna Gerbrandy en dr. mr. Sybe de Vries

Europa Instituut Universiteit Utrecht

eleven international publishing

Published, sold and distributed by Eleven International Publishing
P.O. Box 85576
2508 CG Den Haag
Tel.: +31 70 330 7033
Fax: +31 70-330 7030
e-mail: verkoop@budh.nl
www.elevenpub.com

Sold and distributed in USA and Canada
International Specialized Book Services
920 NE 58th Avenue, Suite 300
Portland, OR 97213-3786, USA
Tel: 1-800-944-6190 (toll-free)
Fax: +1 503 280-8832
orders@isbs.com
www.isbs.com

Printed on acid-free paper.

ISBN: 978-94-90947-11-8

Printed in The Netherlands

Inhoudsopgave

1 Inleiding

Op 12 april 2010 riep Dacian Ciolos, de Europese commissaris voor Landbouw en plattelandsontwikkeling, op tot een publiek debat over de landbouw voor het Europa van morgen.[1] In zijn voordracht worden vier strategische vragen centraal gesteld:

- Waarom een gemeenschappelijk landbouwbeleid?
- Welke doelen stelt de samenleving voor de landbouw in al zijn verscheidenheid?
- Waarom moet het gemeenschappelijk landbouwbeleid worden hervormd en hoe kan het de verwachtingen in de samenleving inlossen?
- Wat zijn de instrumenten voor het gemeenschappelijk landbouwbeleid van morgen?

Het is zeker niet de eerste keer dat de toekomst van het landbouwbeleid in Europa ter discussie staat. Gezien de complexiteit van de landbouwmarkten is dit niet onbegrijpelijk.

Wat de markt voor melk betreft, die in deze bijdrage centraal staat, behelzen de meest recente plannen van de Europese Commissie de beperking van inkomenssteun aan melkveehouders en de afschaffing van melkquota per 2015. Maar zoals commissaris Ciolos in zijn voordracht ook aangaf, vele vragen betreffende de toekomst van de landbouwsector staan nog open. Tegen de achtergrond van deze ontwikkelingen waarbij besloten is om bepaalde interventiemaatregelen niet meer te nemen, is het interessant om te bezien of een vorm van zelfregulering door melkveehouders, al dan niet met steun van de (nationale of Europese) overheid, een alternatief instrument zou kunnen zijn voor de regulering van de Europese markt voor melk. Maar dergelijke initiatieven tot zelfregulering stuiten mogelijk af op de toepassing van Europese en nationale mededingingsregels.

In dit boek staat dan ook de vraag centraal of de Europese landbouwregelgeving en mededingingsregels ruimte laten voor zelfregulering van de melkmarkt. De subvragen daarbij zijn: welke juridische regels zijn van belang en welke vorm van regulering is binnen de huidige regels mogelijk?

In hoofdstuk 2 wordt een korte uiteenzetting over het Europese landbouwbeleid ten aanzien van melkveehouderij gegeven en wordt bezien welke onderdelen daarvan in het bijzonder op bezwaren kunnen stuiten aan de kant van de betrokken landbouwers. Dit betreft vooral de afschaffing van de melkquota. De vrees van de melkveehouders is dat door het afschaffen van melkquota in 2015 de markt instabiel raakt, het prijsniveau wisselend wordt,

---

1 Toespraak voor de Commissie Landbouw van het Europees Parlement, 12 april 2010, SPEECH/10/150, beschikbaar via: http://europa.eu/rapid/pressReleasesAction.do?reference=SPEECH/10/150&format=HTML&aged=1&language=NL&guiLanguage=en.

dat het op dat moment voor melkveehouders niet toereikend zal zijn om kostendekkend te produceren en dat de inkomens te laag zullen zijn voor een stabiele melkveehouderij.

Hoofdstuk 3 gaat in op de vraag of de huidige regels van Europees recht ruimte laten voor zelfregulering. Daarbij wordt met name ingegaan op het Europese mededingingsrecht en de relatie tussen landbouwbeleid en mededingingsbeleid. Zoals zal blijken, is er weliswaar ruimte voor enige vorm van zelfregulering, maar beperkt.

Hoofdstuk 4 behandelt de vraag of de huidige regels zouden kunnen en moeten worden aangepast om zelfregulering te kunnen invoeren. Kort samengevat zal blijken dat daarbij ofwel de uitzonderingen binnen het mededingingsrecht zullen moeten worden opgerekt, ofwel de ruimte binnen het landbouwbeleid moet worden gecreëerd.

In hoofdstuk 5 wordt ten slotte een aantal suggesties gedaan die kunnen leiden tot aanpassing van het landbouw- en mededingingsbeleid, opdat beter rekening gehouden kan worden met de belangen van de melkveehouders.

2 Europees landbouwbeleid

2.1 Juridische basis

a Verdragsbepalingen betreffende de landbouw

Het Europese landbouwbeleid (het gemeenschappelijk landbouwbeleid, of GLB) heeft vanaf het begin van de Europese samenwerking een belangrijke plaats ingenomen in de verdragen. Ook de EEG had expliciet al betrekking op de integratie van landbouwactiviteiten. Dit kan verklaard worden doordat de landbouwmarkten in de lidstaten van oudsher geordend waren in het kader van marktordeningen, dat de toepassing van de vrijverkeerbepalingen deze ordeningen zou ondermijnen en dat dus een gemeenschappelijke markt in deze sector alleen tot stand kon worden gebracht door een totale vergemeenschappelijking van nationaal marktordeningsbeleid.[1] Het landbouwbeleid voorziet dan ook in de meest vergaande vorm van integratie, namelijk een geheel samengaan van negatieve en positieve integratie. Welke maatregelen in het kader van deze gemeenschappelijke politiek precies moeten worden genomen, kon echter niet duidelijk uit het Verdrag worden afgeleid.

Overigens geldt dat in het Verdrag en ook in secundaire regelingen geen duidelijke definitie wordt gegeven van 'landbouwer': dat betekent dat de keuze wie als landbouwer wordt aangemerkt, grotendeels wordt overgelaten aan de lidstaten, die hierin een zekere mate van beoordelingsvrijheid kennen. Deze vraag zou een rol kunnen spelen bij de toepassing van de uitzondering van artikel 106 lid 2 VWEU (zie par. 4.3.3).[2]

Als uitgangspunt voor het landbouwbeleid dienden tot voor kort artikel 2 EG en 3 EG, waarin de doelstellingen en taken van de Europese Gemeenschap waren opgenomen. Het Verdrag van Lissabon, dat op 1 december 2009 in werking is getreden, heeft dit juridisch kader echter gewijzigd. Het EG-Verdrag is opgegaan in het huidige Verdrag betreffende de Werking van de Europese Unie (hierna het EU-Werkingsverdrag), terwijl de doelstel-

---

1 Kapteyn & VerLoren van Themaat, *Het recht van de Europese Unie en van de Europese Gemeenschappen*, Kluwer: Deventer, 2003, p. 970.

2 Zie hierover: J.A. McMahon, *EU Agricultural Law*, Oxford University Press: New York, 2007, p. 2-4. Het is duidelijk dat 'melk' valt onder de bepalingen die betrekking hebben op landbouw, en landbouwbeleid, nu art. 38 VWEU bepaalt: 'Onder landbouwproducten worden verstaan de voortbrengselen van bodem, veeteelt en visserij alsmede de producten in eerste graad van bewerking welke met de genoemde voortbrengselen rechtstreeks verband houden.'

lingen van de Europese Unie in het Verdrag betreffende de Europese Unie (hierna: het EU-Verdrag) staan vermeld.

Het oorspronkelijke artikel 2 EG, dat de taken van de EG weergaf, is in grote lijnen opgegaan in artikel 3 lid 3 VEU, waarin het volgende staat:

> 'De Unie brengt een interne markt tot stand. Zij zet zich in voor de duurzame ontwikkeling van Europa, op basis van een *evenwichtige groei en van prijsstabiliteit, een sociale markteconomie* met een groot concurrentievermogen die gericht is op volledige werkgelegenheid en sociale vooruitgang, en van een *hoog niveau van bescherming en verbetering van de kwaliteit van het milieu.* De Unie bevordert wetenschappelijke en technische vooruitgang.
> [...]
> De Unie bestrijdt sociale uitsluiting en discriminatie, en *bevordert sociale rechtvaardigheid en bescherming* [...].
> De Unie bevordert de *economische, sociale en territoriale samenhang,* en de solidariteit tussen de lidstaten.'[3]

Vervolgens bepaalt artikel 3 lid 6 VEU dat deze doelstellingen met passende middelen worden nagestreefd, naar gelang de bevoegdheden die de Unie zijn toebedeeld in de verdragen.

In artikel 4 lid 2 sub d VWEU wordt het landbouw- en visserijbeleid gekwalificeerd als gedeelde bevoegdheid van de Europese Unie en de lidstaten. Dit betekent volgens artikel 2 lid 2 VWEU dat de Unie en de lidstaten wetgevend kunnen optreden en bindende handelingen kunnen vaststellen. Bovendien oefenen de lidstaten hun bevoegdheid uit voor zover de Unie haar bevoegdheid niet heeft uitgeoefend. Maar juist op het terrein van landbouw heeft de Europese Unie veelvuldig van haar bevoegdheid gebruikgemaakt.

Het landbouwbeleid is verder gebaseerd op de landbouwtitel van het Verdrag. Volgens artikel 38 VWEU bepaalt de Unie een gemeenschappelijk landbouw- en visserijbeleid en voert dat uit. In deze bepaling staat onder meer wat onder landbouwproducten wordt verstaan (onder andere dus melk en afgeleide producten), maar ook – belangrijk voor deze bijdrage – de relatie tussen de interne markt en het landbouwbeleid, waaruit blijkt dat de interne markt ook de landbouw omvat, en dat de regels van de interne markt ook van toepassing zijn op landbouwproducten.[4]

---

3 Cursief is toegevoegd.

4 Art. 38 lid 1, 2 en 4 VWEU: 'De interne markt omvat mede de landbouw en de handel in landbouwproducten. [...] Voor zover in de artikelen 39 tot en met 44 niet anders is bepaald, zijn de regels voor de instelling van de interne markt van toepassing op de landbouwproducten. [...] De werking en de ontwikkeling van de

Artikel 39 VWEU geeft de doelstellingen van het GLB. Het bepaalt:

> '1. Het gemeenschappelijk landbouwbeleid heeft ten doel:
> a. de productiviteit van de landbouw te doen toenemen door de technische vooruitgang te bevorderen en door zowel de rationele ontwikkeling van de landbouwproductie als een optimaal gebruik van de productiefactoren, met name de arbeidskrachten, te verzekeren
> b. aldus de landbouwbevolking een redelijke levensstandaard te verzekeren, met name door de verhoging van het hoofdelijk inkomen van hen die in de landbouw werkzaam zijn;
> c. de markten te stabiliseren;
> d. de voorziening veilig te stellen;
> e. redelijke prijzen bij de levering aan verbruikers te verzekeren.'

Het tweede lid geeft de bijzondere status van landbouw weer:

> 'bij het tot stand brengen van het gemeenschappelijk landbouwbeleid en van de daarvoor te treffen bijzondere voorzieningen zal rekening gehouden worden met: a) de bijzondere aard van het landbouwbedrijf, welke voortvloeit uit de maatschappelijke structuur van de landbouw en uit de structurele en natuurlijke ongelijkheid tussen de verschillende landbouwgebieden; b) de noodzaak de dienstige aanpassingen geleidelijk te doen verlopen; c) het feit, dat de landbouwsector in de lidstaten nauw verweven is met de gehele economie.'

Deze doelstellingen zijn met het Verdrag van Lissabon overigens niet gewijzigd. Om de doelen in artikel 39 te bereiken, wordt het GLB ontwikkeld. De vorm daarvan is voorgeschreven, namelijk in artikel 40 VWEU: 'a) gemeenschappelijke regels inzake mededinging; b) verplichte coördinatie van de verschillende nationale marktorganisaties; c) een Europese marktorganisatie.'

Het tweede lid bepaalt:

> 'de gemeenschappelijke ordening (...) kan alle maatregelen medebrengen welke noodzakelijk zijn om de in artikel 39 omschreven doelstellingen te bereiken, met name prijsregelingen, subsidies zowel voor de productie als voor het in de handel brengen der verschillende producten, systemen van voorraadvorming

---

interne markt voor de landbouwproducten dienen gepaard te gaan met de totstandkoming van een gemeenschappelijk landbouwbeleid.'

> en opslag en gemeenschappelijke organisatorische voorzieningen voor de stabilisatie van de in- of uitvoer'.

De verhouding tussen het mededingingsrecht en het landbouwbeleid is voorwerp van artikel 42 VWEU (zie ook par. 4.1):

> 'De bepalingen van het hoofdstuk over regels betreffende de mededinging zijn op de voortbrenging van en de handel in landbouwproducten slechts in zoverre van toepassing, als door het Europees Parlement en de Raad met inachtneming van de in artikel 39 vermelde doeleinden zal worden bepaald binnen het raam van de bepalingen en overeenkomstig de procedure van artikel 43 lid 2. De Raad kan, op voorstel van de Commissie, met name machtiging geven tot het verlenen van steun:
> a) ter bescherming van door structurele of natuurlijke omstandigheden benadeelde bedrijven;
> b) in het kader van economische ontwikkelingsplannen.'

De laatste twee artikelen over landbouw betreffen enkele institutionele bepalingen. Hierop wordt in deze bijdrage verder niet ingegaan. Wel van belang om op te merken is dat het Europees Parlement (eindelijk) op basis van artikel 43 VWEU een recht van medebeslissing op het terrein van landbouw krijgt.

Deze artikelen van het EU-Verdrag en EU-Werkingsverdrag vormen de basis van het GLB en geven de eventuele ruimte aan voor afwijking van de algemene mededingingsbepalingen. Zij worden wel uitgelegd als uiting gevende aan drie componenten van het landbouwbeleid:

a. de politiek-economische component, waarbij landbouw bijdraagt aan de economische groei;
b. de sociaal-politieke component, waaronder zorg voor de plattelandspopulatie, inclusief een stabiel inkomen, en het plattelandsbeleid (*rural development*), dat meer recent een nieuwe impuls heeft gekregen;
c. de sociaaleconomische component, die de voedselvoorziening van consumenten betreft.[5]

De onderlinge hiërarchie van deze elementen staat echter niet vast: de Europese Commissie dient zorg te dragen voor onderlinge afstemming tussen de doelstellingen, waarbij tijdelijk voorrang mag worden gegeven aan de ene doelstelling boven de andere. Een andere vorm waarin over landbouwbeleid wordt gesproken, is als bestaande uit 'twee pijlers': de eerste

---

5 Zie bijv. J.A. McMahon 2007, p. 21 (zie noot 2 van dit hoofdstuk); J.S. Marsh & P.J. Swanney, *Agriculture and the European Community*, Londen: Allen and Unwin 1980.

pijler omvat de gemeenschappelijke marktordening; de tweede pijler omvat verschillende vormen van steun, maar steeds gerelateerd aan specifieke investeringen, situaties, diensten of activiteiten van de landbouwer.

b Overige verdragsbepalingen die relevant zijn voor het GLB en het mededingingsbeleid

Naast de bovengenoemde bepalingen die specifiek betrekking hebben op het Europese landbouwbeleid, bevat het EU-Werkingsverdrag bepalingen die in het algemeen van belang zijn voor het Europese recht en beleid, dus ook voor het landbouw- en mededingingsbeleid. Zo moeten volgens artikel 11 VWEU de eisen inzake milieubescherming worden geïntegreerd in de omschrijving en uitvoering van het beleid en het optreden van de Unie, in het bijzonder met het oog op het bevorderen van duurzame ontwikkeling.
Verder bepaalt artikel 13 VWEU het volgende:

> 'Bij het formuleren en uitvoeren van het beleid van de Unie op het gebied van landbouw, visserij [...]houden de Unie en de lidstaten ten volle rekening met hetgeen vereist is voor het welzijn van dieren als wezens met gevoel, onder eerbiediging van de wettelijke en bestuursrechtelijke bepalingen en gebruiken van de lidstaten met betrekking tot met name godsdienstige riten, culturele tradities en regionaal erfgoed.'

Daarnaast is mogelijk ook de integratiebepaling uit de cultuurtitel van belang, artikel 167 lid 4 VWEU, die bepaalt dat de Unie bij haar optreden rekening houdt met culturele aspecten, met name de culturele verscheidenheid.

Ook al is onduidelijk welke precieze juridische effecten deze integratiebepalingen met zich brengen, het belang van deze bepalingen mag niet onderschat worden. Ze staan immers in Titel II van het EU-Werkingsverdrag onder 'algemeen toepasselijke bepalingen' en begrenzen de discretionaire bevoegdheid van de instellingen van de Europese Unie in die zin dat in het kader van het landbouw- of mededingingsbeleid rekening gehouden moet worden met milieubelangen, het belang van dierenwelzijn of culturele aspecten.[6] Deze aspecten van het gemeenschappelijk landbouwbeleid worden hiermee versterkt. Tegelijkertijd zullen de Europese Commissie, het Gerecht en het Hof van Justitie in de toepassing en handhaving van de Europese mededingingsregels ook rekening moeten houden met deze belangen. Overigens voert de Europese Commissie voor de belangrijkste wetgevingsinitiatieven een effectrapportage uit, waarbij de sociale, economische en milieueffecten

6 Zie ook S.A. de Vries, *Tensions within the Internal Market – The Functioning of the Internal Market and the Development of Horizontal and Flanking Policies*, Groningen: Europa Law Publishing, 2006, p. 18-19.

van wetgevingsvoorstellen worden beoordeeld.[7] Hierna wordt hierop verder ingegaan (zie par. 4.3).

Ten slotte is artikel 14 VWEU over diensten van algemeen economisch belang mogelijk van belang voor de verhouding tussen het landbouwbeleid en het mededingingsrecht.

2.2 Ontwikkelingen

Het GLB is een groot succes geworden, maar ging aan dat succes bijna ten onder: overproductie was het gevolg. Een proces van hervormingen volgde, ook in de melksector. Zo werden in 1984 quota en heffingen geïntroduceerd.[8] Daardoor nam het productieoverschot echter niet af. De quota werden derhalve verlaagd.[9] Het quotasysteem heeft geleid tot vele rechtszaken, maar is door het Hof van Justitie steeds in principe goedgekeurd als maatregel om vraag en aanbod met elkaar in balans te brengen. Dat is van belang, omdat daarmee het systeem als zodanig niet in strijd is met het Verdrag.[10]

Al in 1991 werd een begin gemaakt met een fundamentele hervorming van het GLB: de onderlinge verhouding tussen de genoemde componenten werd geherstructureerd, waarbij bescherming van het milieu, in het kader van plattelandsontwikkeling, aan belang won. Deze hervorming heeft geleid tot het introduceren van algemene maatregelen, waarbij boeren werden gecompenseerd voor milieuvriendelijke maatregelen. Daarbij werden bijvoorbeeld landbouwers gestimuleerd land opzij te zetten voor andere doeleinden dan landbouw. Het is van belang om op te merken dat de serie regelingen die deze nieuwe route onderbouwden, niet alleen gericht was op het stimuleren van milieuvriendelijkheid, maar ook op het stimuleren van ondernemerschap, zodat boeren voor hun inkomen niet alleen afhankelijk zouden zijn van de landbouwactiviteiten. In 2000 werden deze hervormingen geëvalueerd in de Agenda 2000.[11] Daarin wordt de hervorming een succes genoemd, omdat zij heeft geleid tot meer marktbalans en (gemiddeld) hogere inkomens. Tegelijkertijd blijken de resultaten voor het milieu meer gemengd.[12]

---

7 Te vinden op <http://ec.europa.eu/governance/impact/index_en.htm>.

8 Bij Verordening (EEG) nr. 856/84 van de Raad tot wijziging van Verordening (EEG) nr. 804/68 houdende een gemeenschappelijke ordening der markten in de sector melk en zuivelproducten, Pb. EG L 90 van 31 maart 1984, p. 10.

9 Verordeningen 1355/86, Pb. EG L 118 van 7 mei 1986, p. 1 en 777/87, Pb. EG L 78 van 20 maart 1987, p. 10. Het uiteindelijke systeem werd neergelegd in Verordening 3950/92, Pb. EG L 405 van 31 december 1992, p. 1.

10 Zie, bijvoorbeeld, zaak 44/79, Jur. 1979, p. 3727 (*Hauer*); zaak 5/88, *Jur.* 1989, p. 2609 (*Wachauf*)p. 2609.

11 Agenda 2000, A CAP for the future, <http://ec.europa.eu/agriculture/publi/review99/08_09_en.pdf>.

12 McMahon 2007, p. 98 (zie noot 2 van dit hoofdstuk).

De Agenda 2000 bevat ook een programma voor verdere hervormingen: waar het landbouwbeleid lang gebaseerd is geweest op productiesteun, waardoor boeren werden gestimuleerd *meer* te produceren, wordt nu op andere wijze gestuurd: *output driven*. Daarbij werd aan boeren directe inkomenssteun verleend (in plaats van op productie), maar werden ook eisen gesteld aan de wijze van productie, kwaliteit en beheer. Bovendien werd hier voorgesteld de quota voor melk gefaseerd af te schaffen. Daarnaast bevat de Agenda 2000 de verdere ontwikkeling van het plattelandsbeleid: meer aandacht voor de sociale aspecten van het platteland, en meer aandacht voor milieu.

Veel van de maatregelen die werden voorgesteld in de Agenda 2000 zijn ondertussen (al dan niet in gewijzigde vorm) geïntroduceerd, waaronder de gefaseerde afschaffing van de melkquota (uiteindelijk af te schaffen in 2015). In 2002 volgde de *mid-term review*,[13] naar aanleiding waarvan (onder andere) het *single payment scheme* (SPS) werd geïntroduceerd: een steun in de vorm van een jaarlijkse inkomensuitkering, waarbij de uitkering werd gekoppeld aan voorschriften ten aanzien van ecologisch beleid (de *cross-compliance*). Uiteindelijk worden de *single payments* echter ook gefaseerd afgeschaft. In 2007 lanceerde de Commissie de zogenoemde *health-check* van de hervorming van het landbouwbeleid,[14] die in 2009 werd herhaald.[15] Daarbij wordt de hervorming van het landbouwbeleid geëvalueerd, en worden (nog) verdere voorstellen gedaan voor versimpeling van regelgeving (onder andere de algemene gemeenschappelijke marktordening) en implementatie in de lidstaten.[16]

2.3 De bijzondere eigenschappen van de melkmarkt

De voorgestelde afschaffing van quota heeft tot verzet geleid, dat met name samenhangt met de huidige, historisch lage melkprijs.[17] Zo menen de Nederlandse melkveehouders verenigd in de Nederlandse Melkveehouders Vakbond, dat met de afschaffing van elke productieregulering de stabiliteit van de melkvoorziening, de inkomsten voor de melkveehouders, en de instandhouding van het platteland in gevaar komen. De schommelingen

13 COM(2002)394, def.

14 COM(2007)722, def.

15 Te vinden op <http://ec.europa.eu/agriculture/healthcheck/index_en.htm>.

16 De huidige gemeenschappelijke ordening is neergelegd in Verordening 1787/2003 van de Raad van 29 september 2003 tot wijziging van Verordening 1255/1999 houdende een gemeenschappelijke ordening der markten in de sector melk en zuivelproducten. Die is een aantal malen gewijzigd. Zie voor een overzicht van geldende maatregelen: <http://eur-lex.europa.eu/en/legis/latest/chap0360.htm>.

17 Informatie over de protesten van de Nederlandse melkveehouders, de Franse en Spaanse boeren, is bijvoorbeeld te vinden via: <www.voorwie.eu/ec-en-handel/270-europese-commissie-blijft-bij-afschaffing-melkquota-melkveehouders-willen-juist-een-duurzaam-en-flexibel-quotasysteem.html>.

in de marktprijs voor melk van de afgelopen jaren zijn hiervoor een indicatie. Binnen een jaar bereikte de melkprijs het hoogste (50 cent) en het laagste (20 cent) niveau, gezien over de afgelopen 30 jaar. Er zijn enkele economische redenen waarom de markt voor melk niet een gewone markt is, waarin de melkproductie en prijsbepaling geheel aan het marktmechanisme dient te worden overgelaten. Het belangrijkste argument dat in dit verband naar voren wordt gebracht, is dat het voor de individuele melkveehouders onmogelijk is om de markt te reguleren, in die zin dat de marktprikkels niet goed werken. Een individuele melkveehouder heeft geen invloed op de totale productie van de markt en zal zowel in een situatie van algemeen productietekort als algemeen productieoverschot zijn productie uitbreiden: in een tekortsituatie, met een hoge melkprijs, breidt hij uit om zijn winst te verhogen; in een overschotsituatie, met een lage melkprijs, zal hij uitbreiden om de efficiëntie te verhogen en de kosten te verlagen. Zelfs met de uiterst lage melkprijs van 2009 is de melkproductie uitgebreid, waardoor het overschot slechts toeneemt, in plaats van dat het aanbod aangepast wordt aan de verminderde vraag.

Er zijn echter bijkomende argumenten die kunnen worden gebruikt ter ondersteuning van het betoog waarom de markt voor melk geen 'gewone' markt is, zoals het feit dat melk *basisvoedsel* vormt, en de verbinding van de melkproductie (de melkveehouderijen) met het aanzicht van het platteland en het belang van het platteland als recreatie-, woon-, en leefgebied voor een groot deel van de bevolking. In Nederland, maar wellicht ook in andere EU-lidstaten, staat het traditionele cultuurlandschap met de koe in de wei steeds meer onder druk. Daarnaast kan de melkveehouder een belangrijke rol spelen bij het natuurbehoud.

De Commissaris voor landbouw heeft echter vooralsnog aangegeven niets te zien in het herformuleren van quota, maar de oplossing van de lage inkomens van melkveehouders te zien in andere maatregelen, waarvan een heel aantal reeds bestaand. In juni 2010 is een 'Groep op hoog niveau' (*High Level Group*) met zeven aanbevelingen voor de zuivelsector van de EU gekomen.[18] Deze groep is op initiatief van de Commissaris voor landbouw in 2009 opgericht om, naar aanleiding van het verstrijken van de melkquota op 1 april 2015, regelingen op middellange en lange termijn te bespreken en te bekijken welke maatregelen bevorderlijk kunnen zijn voor de marktstabiliteit, de producenteninkomens en de markttransparantie. Overigens heeft ook DG Mededinging van de Europese Commissie een bijdrage aan het verslag gegeven. De Commissie is voornemens om voor het einde van dit jaar wetgevingsvoorstellen in te dienen met als doel een betere structurering van de gehele sector. De aanbevelingen van de 'Groep op hoog niveau' hebben betrekking op:

18 IP/10/742, Brussel, 15 juni 2010.

- *contractuele betrekkingen* tussen de melkproducenten en de melkverwerkers, waarbij vooraf een schriftelijk contract wordt gesloten over de levering van rauwe melk met bepalingen over prijs, hoeveelheid, tijdschema en looptijd, eventueel opgelegd door de lidstaat;
- *collectieve onderhandelingspositie van de producenten*, om gezamenlijk met een zuivelbedrijf te kunnen onderhandelen over hun contractuele voorwaarden, inclusief de prijs;
- *rol van de brancheorganisaties*, die vergelijkbaar zou kunnen zijn met de brancheorganisaties in de groente- en fruitsector;
- *transparantie in de zuivelbevoorradingsketen;*
- *marktmaatregelen, handelsnormen en oorsprongsetikettering*; en
- *innovatie en onderzoek.*

Bij het afronden van dit boek is de Commissie inderdaad met een voorstel voor een verordening gekomen, gericht op de versterking van de positie van de melkproducenten in de zuivelbevoorradingsketen en op een meer marktgerichte en duurzame toekomst. Het voorstel van de Commissie incorporeert een aantal bevindingen uit dit boek. Maar de Commissie geeft ook aan dat er geen redenen bestaan voor een herziening van de in het kader van de gezondheidscontrole ('health check') genomen besluiten over een geleidelijke verhoging van de quota en de afschaffing van de quotaregeling op 1 april 2015.[19]

Buiten Europa kennen we vormen van zelfregulering in de melksector die goed functioneren. In het rapport van de 'Groep op hoog niveau' zijn vier landen van buiten de EU gevraagd om hun marktorganisaties te beschrijven: de Verenigde Staten, Zwitserland, Australië en Nieuw-Zeeland. Deze landen kennen allemaal uitzonderingen voor melkveehouders van de mededingingsregels, hoewel de reikwijdte van de uitzonderingen per land verschilt.[20] De Nederlandse melkveehouders verwijzen graag naar de regeling die in Canada van toepassing is en die is vormgegeven volgens de volgende principes:
- De Canadese boeren hebben zich aangesloten bij zogenaamde *pooling systems.* Zes provincies hebben zich geconcentreerd in de *Agreement on All Milk Pooling* (P5). De overige vier provincies hebben zich geconcentreerd in de *Western Milk Pooling Agreement.*
- Deze *pooling systems* zorgen ervoor dat de melkboeren de mogelijkheid hebben om hun opbrengsten, markten en sommige onkosten te delen. Bij een van de twee afspraken gaat men zelfs zo ver dat de boeren al hun inkomsten delen, zodat iedereen dezelfde

19 Voorstel voor een verordening tot wijziging van Verordening (EG) nr. 1234/2007 met betrekking tot contractuele betrekkingen in de zuivel- en zuivelproductensector COM(2010)728; zie ook Persbericht IP/10/1691, Brussel, 9 december 2010.

20 Zie ook: Report of the High Level Group on Milk, final version 15 June 2010, p. 11.

prijs ontvangt voor zijn/haar melk. Doordat de markten gedeeld worden, is het mogelijk dat indien er sprake is van een stijging van de vraag in provincie A, de boeren uit de overige provincies melk kunnen leveren om hieraan te voldoen. Bij deze afspraak delen de melkveehouders naast de inkomsten ook de kosten voor vervoer en promotie.

- Het is vervolgens aan de *Canadian Dairy Commission* om er door middel van een nationaal *supply management*-systeem voor te zorgen dat er geen sprake is van overproductie. Zij berekent aan de hand van de door de *provincial milk boards* maandelijks toegezonden informatie hoeveel melk er per provincie geproduceerd dient te worden om te voldoen aan de vraag. Dit wordt gedurende het jaar in de gaten gehouden en zo nodig aangepast. Naast de vaststelling van de prijs van de melk, stelt zij per jaar de prijzen voor boter en mageremelkpoeder vast.

Geconcludeerd kan worden dat de Canadese regeling inhoudt dat boeren zijn gekomen tot zelfregulering, maar met goedkeuring van de overheid. Er is sprake van quotering, in de zin van productieregeling, en van prijsbinding, in de zin van opgelegde prijzen voor melk op de markt. Daarbij is een forse investering gedaan in een systeem dat dit alles moet reguleren.[21]

Ook de Europese melkveehouders willen *zelf* de markt kunnen reguleren, zodat marktgericht geproduceerd kan worden en melkveehouders door middel van een kostendekkende melkprijs hun inkomen uit de markt kunnen halen. Zij zijn dan niet meer afhankelijk van subsidies en toeslagen van de overheid. Deze kunnen verminderd of zelfs afgeschaft worden. De zelfregulering moet echter wel worden ingebed in een wettelijk raamwerk van de overheid. In Frankrijk is een eerste stap gezet in de richting van samenwerking tussen melkveehouders en leveranciers van melkproducten door een stijging van de melkprijzen af te spreken. De Franse overheid wil de melksector indexeren en zich actief bezighouden met het markt- en prijsbeleid van de melksector in Frankrijk. Binnen een nationaal wettelijk raamwerk worden verticale prijsafspraken afgesproken, waarbij het aantal producenten dat in vereniging mag onderhandelen, verhoogd wordt van vierhonderd naar vierduizend. De Franse minister van Landbouw wil daarbij zover gaan als mogelijk is binnen het kader van het Europese mededingingsrecht.[22] De vraag is uiteraard of de Europese mededingingsregels, waarop hierna wordt ingegaan, dergelijke afspraken wel toestaan.

---

21 Zie voor informatie over het Canadese systeem onder andere: <www.voorwie.eu/nieuws/271-europese-commissie-houdt-vast-aan-afschaffing-melkquota-melkveehouders-willen-een-duurzaam-en-flexibel-quotasysteem.html>.

22 Zie voor het verslag van de Commissie Economie in de Franse Senaat: *Compte Rendu Intégral* du Senat, Séance du mardi 27 avril 2010, *Journal Officiel de la République Francaise*, n. 35 S. (C.R.) 2010, p. 2832.

3 Mededingingsrecht en landbouwbeleid na Lissabon

3.1 Het Verdrag van Lissabon en het EU-mededingingsbeleid

Sinds de inwerkingtreding van het Verdrag van Lissabon staat het begrip 'onvervalste mededinging' niet meer in de doelstellingencatalogus van het Verdrag. Het oude artikel 2 EG noemde het waarborgen van onvervalste mededinging als centrale taak om de doelstellingen van de Europese Gemeenschap te verwezenlijken. Deze taak komt in het huidige artikel 3 EU niet meer terug. In plaats daarvan is een protocol aan het Verdrag gehecht, Protocol Nr. 27, waarin staat dat 'de interne markt als omschreven in artikel 3 [...] een regime omvat dat verzekert dat de mededinging niet wordt verstoord [...]'.

Dat mededinging niet meer expliciet genoemd staat in de doelstellingen van de Europese Unie, wordt vooral aan de Franse president Sarkozy toegeschreven, die hiermee wilde benadrukken – en waarschijnlijk tegelijkertijd de Fransen geruststellen – dat de Europese Unie niet slechts een procompetitief en neoliberaal marktmodel voorstaat. Maar aangezien een protocol dezelfde juridische status heeft als het Verdrag, is het de vraag wat de precieze betekenis van deze wijziging in de doelstellingen uiteindelijk is.

Het belang van een bepaling als artikel 3 EU, waarin de doelstellingen en taken van de Europese Unie staan opgesomd, moet tegelijkertijd niet onderschat worden. In verschillende uitspraken heeft het Hof van Justitie verwezen naar het oude artikel 3 lid 1(g) EG en hieraan inspiratie ontleend ter ondersteuning van het fundamentele karakter van de mededingingsbepalingen.[1] Het feit dat onvervalste mededinging niet in artikel 3 EU is opgenomen en dat tegelijkertijd een nieuw begrip, namelijk 'sociale markteconomie', in artikel 3 EU wordt geïntroduceerd, zou in ieder geval moeten betekenen dat sociale en andere belangen, zoals milieu, een nadrukkelijker rol spelen in het marktintegratieproces en dat bij de toepassing van de mededingingsbepalingen ook aan dergelijke belangen gewicht wordt toegekend (zie hierna, par. 4.3).[2]

---

1 Zie, bijvoorbeeld, zaak C-67/96, *Jur.* 1999, p. I-5751 (*Albany*); zaak C-453/99, *Jur.* 2001, p. I-6297 (*Courage*).

2 Zie F. Amtenbrink & J. van de Gronden, 'Economisch Recht en het Verdrag van Lissabon I – mededinging en interne markt', *SEW*, 2008, p. 325.

3.2 De verbodsbepalingen

Voor de toepasselijkheid van de mededingingsregels op de landbouwsector is het allereerst van belang te bepalen of deze regels ook gelden voor landbouwers in het algemeen en melkveehouders in het bijzonder. De mededingingsregels gelden voor ondernemingen. Ondernemingen zijn, volgens de rechtspraak van het Hof van Justitie EU (hierna: Hof), entiteiten die een economische activiteit uitoefenen, bestaande uit het aanbieden van goederen en diensten op de markt.[3] Landbouwbedrijven en melkveehouders vallen onder dit begrip, ook als het gaat om individuele boeren: zij bieden hun producten aan op de markt, oefenen een economische activiteit uit, en zijn daarmee onderneming in de zin van het mededingingsrecht. Het doet niet ter zake dat er volgens het nationale vennootschapsrecht, bijvoorbeeld, geen sprake is van een onderneming.

De belangrijkste regels zijn vervolgens het *kartelverbod* en het *verbod op het maken van misbruik van een machtspositie.* Dat laatste verbod is neergelegd in artikel 102 VWEU. Het misbruikverbod betekent dat een dominante onderneming – een onderneming, of groep ondernemingen, die een positie hebben van meer dan 40 procent op de markt heeft al snel een dominante positie – van die positie geen misbruik mag maken door, bijvoorbeeld, te lage of te hoge prijzen te vragen of concurrenten van de markt te drukken. Dit verbod zou voor melkveehouders wellicht relevant kunnen zijn in de relatie tussen de individuele (of collectieve) boeren en de supermarkten, maar heeft voor het huidige onderwerp minder relevantie.

Het kartelverbod is neergelegd in artikel 101 VWEU. De hoofdregels van mededingingsrecht in de Nederlandse en de EU-context zijn overigens vrijwel gelijk. Dat komt omdat de Nederlandse Mededingingswet, die sinds 1998 geldt, is gebaseerd op de EU-regels. In het hiernavolgende wordt vooral stilgestaan bij de Europese mededingingsregels. Artikel 101 VWEU bepaalt dat verboden zijn:

> 'alle overeenkomsten tussen ondernemingen, alle besluiten van ondernemersverenigingen en alle onderling afgestemde feitelijke gedragingen welke de handel tussen lidstaten ongunstig kunnen beïnvloeden en ertoe strekken of ten gevolge hebben dat de mededinging binnen de interne markt wordt verhinderd, beperkt of vervalst'.

Daarbij gelden specifieke interpretaties van de begrippen. Zo is het begrip 'overeenkomst' veel ruimer dan alleen een ondertekend contract. Het begrip 'onderling afgestemde feitelijke

3 Zaak C-41/90, *Jur.* 1991, p. I-01979 (*Höfner*) .

gedragingen' betekent dat bovendien ook als er geen sprake is van een overeenkomst, er nog steeds sprake kan zijn van verboden afstemming van gedrag.[4] Het begrip 'ondernemersvereniging' omvat zowel formele verenigingen als meer informele verbanden, en omvat in ieder geval brancheorganisaties zoals, bijvoorbeeld, een melkveehoudersvakbond. Een 'besluit' van een ondernemersvereniging is elke handeling waarvan een zekere binding uitgaat. Een regeling, uitgaande van een nationale of overkoepelende Europese vereniging van melkveehouders, over productie en prijzen zou zeker onder de reikwijdte van het verbod vallen.

Het gaat bij het kartelverbod om afspraken die de *mededinging* beperken. Het artikel zelf geeft een aantal voorbeelden: zo zijn prijsafspraken (aankoopprijs of verkoopprijs) verboden, en ook quoteringsafspraken of afspraken die 'bestaan in het beperken of controleren van de productie, de afzet, de technische ontwikkeling of de investeringen', en marktverdelingafspraken. Daarbij geldt dat de afspraak de mededinging 'merkbaar' moet beperken. Dit betekent dat als de impact op de markt klein is – doordat de ondernemingen klein zijn of een gering marktaandeel hebben – het verbod niet geldt. Voor de toepassing van de Europese mededingingsregels is dan de bagatelbekendmaking, ook wel *de minimis*-bekendmaking, van de Europese Commissie van belang. Deze wordt in paragraaf 4.2 besproken.

Ten slotte is voor de toepassing van de mededingingsregels uit het Verdrag van belang dat de handel tussen lidstaten is beïnvloed. In het klassieke arrest *Grundig/Consten* interpreteert het Hof van Justitie deze voorwaarde als volgt: de overeenkomst kan direct of indirect, daadwerkelijk dan wel slechts potentieel, de vrije handel tussen de lidstaten beïnvloeden.[5]

Quota en heffingen

Een regeling naar voorbeeld van de Canadese regeling, waarbij door de boeren in een samenwerkingsverband – of door een instantie die boven de boeren staat, maar waarbij de boeren zich aansluiten – *quota* worden afgesproken, en *prijzen* bepaald, is in beginsel in strijd met dit verbod op het maken van mededingingsbeperkende afspraken. Prijsafspraken in horizontale relaties en quoteringsregelingen zijn bovendien hardcoreafspraken, waarvan wordt uitgegaan dat zij vrijwel altijd onder het kartelverbod zullen vallen.

---

4 Gev. zaken 48-69-57/69, *Jur.* 1972, p. 619 (*ICI v. Commissie (Kleurstoffen)*), r.o. 64.

5 Gev. zaken 56 en 58/64, *Jur.* 1966, p. 299 (*Consten en Grundig*). Zie ook annotatie A. Gerbrandy, in: T.W.B. Beukers, H.J. van Harten & S. Prechal, *Het recht van de Europese Unie in 50 klassieke arresten*, Den Haag: Boom Juridische uitgevers 2010, p. 30-31. Zie ook: A. Gerbrandy, 'Case Note, Case C-8/08, T-Mobile Netherlands BV, KPN Mobile NV, Orange Nederland NV, Vodafone Libertel NV v. Raad van bestuur van de Nederlandse Mededingingsautoriteit, Judgment of the Court (Third Chamber) of 4 June 2009', *Common Market Law Review* 2010-47, p. 1199-1220.

Het is daarbij belangrijk om op te merken dat het kartelverbod dat prijsafspraken omvat, niet alleen gaat over de 'hele' prijs van een product. Ook een opgelegde heffing, toeslag of bijdrage, die een (klein) deel van de prijs betreft,[6] waarbij het de ondernemingen voor het overige vrijstaat de prijs te bepalen, is een prijsafspraak en daarmee in beginsel verboden. Bovendien, ook als het gaat om 'vrijwillige' bijdragen is er een grote kans dat zij een verboden prijsafspraak is, in de zin van het mededingingsrecht, tenzij er daadwerkelijk sprake is van vrijwilligheid. Dat laatste is bijvoorbeeld niet het geval wanneer de bijdragen verbonden zijn aan kiesrechten zoals neergelegd in de statuten van de organisatie, of wanneer een aanbeveling van het bestuur door haar leden als bindend wordt beschouwd.

Daarnaast kunnen heffingen per eenheid melk, bedoeld om het aanbod te reguleren, weliswaar via een omweg gezien worden als een productiebeperking. Weliswaar staat het huidige mededingingsrecht een 'economische benadering' van overeenkomsten voor waarbij een beoordeling van de afspraak in de economische en juridische context waarin zij vorm heeft gekregen vooropstaat, maar prijsafspraken en productiebeperkingen vormen nog steeds de kern van het verbod. In deze economische benadering staat, meer dan bij marktintegratie, consumentenwelvaart als doelstelling van mededingingsbeleid centraal.[7]

Dit betekent in zekere zin een versoepeling van de beoordeling van afspraken: in plaats van dat de Commissie of de nationale mededingingsautoriteiten afgaan op een etiket van een afspraak, wordt gekeken naar het effect daarvan op de markt. Toch biedt deze economische benadering weinig kans als het gaat om het verkopen van het onderling afspreken van quota of (onderdelen) van de prijs: hardcoreafspraken zullen ook met de economische benadering zelden zijn geoorloofd. Bovendien heeft het Hof van Justitie in recente rechtspraak dit 'beoordelingschema' bevestigd.[8]

Alternatieven, zoals een richtprijs en informatiestromen

De vraag is of bij het gebruik van zelfregulering door melkveehouders alternatieven voorhanden zijn die de mededinging in mindere mate kunnen beperken. Voorstellen die door

6 Besluit NMa, zaak 51, 18 december 1998 en 31 mei 1999 (*Stibat*). Zie ook de VOTOB-beschikking van de Europese Commissie (XXIInd Competition Report 1992), die gezien wordt als een gemiste kans voor de Commissie om milieuoverwegingen in haar beschikkingspraktijk te integreren: F.O.W. Vogelaar, 'Towards an Improved Integration of EC Environmental Policy and EC Competition Policy: An Interim Report', in: B.E. Hawk (Ed.), *Annual Proceedings of the Fordham Corporate Law Institute – International Antitrust Law & Policy 1994*, The Hague: Kluwer Law International 1995, p. 554.

7 Zie, bijvoorbeeld, de literatuur met betrekking tot de Chicago School: R.H. Bork, *The Antitrust Paradox: A Policy at War with Itself*, New York: Basic Books 1978 en A. Jones & B. Sufrin, *EC Competition Law*, Oxford: Oxford University Press, 2008, p. 28-30.

8 Zaak C-8/08, Jur. 2009, p. I-4529 *(T-Mobile)*; zie ook annotatie Gerbrandy 2010, p. 34 (zie noot 5 van dit hoofdstuk).

Nederlandse melkveehouders zijn gedaan bevatten, naast productiebeperkingen in de vorm van quota en heffingen, ook richtprijzen en, noodzakelijk voor de marktanalyse die door het Monitoringsinstituut moet worden ondernomen, informatievergaring. Deze beide onderdelen van de regeling zijn niet direct als hardcorebeperking te kwalificeren. Desalniettemin kunnen zij mededingingsbeperkend zijn in hun *effect*. Ook effectbeperkingen, afspraken die niet ten doel hebben de mededinging te beperken, maar door hun uitwerking in de economische en juridische context waarin zij vorm krijgen, wel dat effect *kunnen* hebben, zijn verboden. Een richtprijs kan een dergelijk effect hebben, omdat zij, in deze context, kan gaan functioneren als minimumprijs of onderlinge prijsafspraak. Hoewel een richtprijs bedoeld kan zijn als bepaling van het moment van ingrijpen (het plegen van een interventie in de markt), kan zij voor marktdeelnemers een bijkomende rol vervullen. Of dat het geval is, zou onderzocht moeten worden.[9]

Wat de informatiestromen betreft: het delen van marktgevoelige informatie kan problematisch zijn, vooral als het gaat om het delen van informatie over hoeveelheden productie, over prijszetting of over nieuwe ontwikkelingen tussen ondernemingen die elkaars concurrenten zijn. Dit is met name het geval in oligopolistische markten, waarin informatie-*uitwisseling* tussen concurrenten de concurrentiestructuur kan verzwakken, ook als deze plaats heeft in een boven de ondernemingen geplaatst instituut of orgaan. Hoewel wij in abstracto moeilijk kunnen beoordelen of de informatiestromen binnen een Monitoringsinstituut, of van een instituut naar de melkveehouders, als beperking is te kwalificeren, is dit iets om rekening mee te houden.

Samenhang

Omdat de quota en de heffing in beginsel duidelijk mededingingsbeperkend zijn, hebben zij in het navolgende vooral de aandacht. Dat neemt niet weg dat de andere mogelijke beperkingen een belangrijke rol kunnen spelen. Daar komt bij dat wanneer een regeling verschillende onderdelen als productiebeperkingen en richtprijzen bevat, deze onderdelen ook *als geheel* dienen te worden beschouwd, omdat ze elkaar ondersteunen en eventueel versterken. Op de vraag of een vorm van zelfregulering toch niet onder het kartelverbod 'uit kan vallen', vanwege de *doelstellingen* die zij nastreeft, wordt hierna in paragraaf 4.3 verder ingegaan.

9 Zie, bijvoorbeeld, wat betreft verticale overeenkomsten: Jones & Sufrin 2008, p. 750 (zie noot 7 van dit hoofdstuk).

3.3 Uitzonderingen

Binnen het mededingingsrecht is een aantal uitzonderingen van kracht die gelden als uitzondering op de verbodsbepaling van artikel 101 lid 1 VWEU. Bij een beroep op deze uitzonderingen is het uitgangspunt dat het mededingingsrecht *wel* van toepassing is, en het verbod in principe ook, maar dat er binnen het mededingingsrecht ruimte is voor afwijking van het kartelverbod van 101 VWEU. Dat is anders bij de uitzondering die te maken heeft met de verhouding tussen landbouwbeleid en mededingingsrecht, waarbij het mededingingsrecht in het geheel niet van toepassing is (zie par. 4.1).

Artikel 101 lid 3 VWEU

De eerste uitzondering die in aanmerking komt, is het derde lid van artikel 101 VWEU. Dit bepaalt:

> 'De bepalingen van lid 1 van dit artikel kunnen echter buiten toepassing worden verklaard voor elke overeenkomst of groep van overeenkomsten tussen ondernemingen, voor elk besluit of groep van besluiten van ondernemersverenigingen, en voor elke onderling afgestemde feitelijke gedraging of groep van gedragingen die
> (1). [10] bijdragen tot verbetering van de productie of van de verdeling der producten of tot verbetering van de technische of economische vooruitgang,
> (2). mits een billijk aandeel in de daaruit voortvloeiende voordelen de gebruikers ten goede komt, en zonder nochtans aan de betrokken ondernemingen
> (3). a) beperkingen op te leggen welke voor het bereiken van deze doelstellingen niet onmisbaar zijn,
> (4). b) de mogelijkheid te geven, voor een wezenlijk deel van de betrokken producten de mededinging uit te schakelen.'

Dit betekent dat als aan de vier genummerde voorwaarden is voldaan, het verbod niet van toepassing is (en dus dat de afspraak toch wel is toegestaan). De Commissie heeft deze vier voorwaarden in een bekendmaking uitgewerkt.[11] Op deze uitzondering wordt hieronder verder ingegaan, met name in het kader van de publieke belangen waarop wellicht een beroep kan worden gedaan (zie par. 4.3.2).

---

10 Cursieve nummers van de voorwaarden zijn toegevoegd.

11 Zie Bekendmaking Commissie toepassing art. 81 lid 3 EG, Pb. EU C 101 van 27 april 2004, p. 97-118.

Artikel 106 lid 2 VWEU

Een andere uitzondering die zou kunnen worden ingeroepen, is de uitzondering voor ondernemingen belast met een dienst van algemeen economisch belang. Deze uitzondering is neergelegd in artikel 106 lid 2 VWEU en geldt voor ondernemingen die belast zijn met een dienst van algemeen economisch belang. De randvoorwaarden voor inroepen zijn dat het moet gaan om:

- belast zijn door de overheid; daarvoor is een actie nodig van die overheid, bijvoorbeeld een besluit, een wet, een regeling;
- een dienst van algemeen economisch belang; dit zijn activiteiten die door de overheid als zodanig worden aangemerkt, zoals nutsvoorzieningen, basistelefonie dienst, basispostdienst, etc.
- het voldoen aan het proportionaliteitsvereiste: de mededingingsregels zijn slechts dan niet van toepassing, als de onderneming zijn dienst van algemeen economisch belang niet kan uitoefenen.

Ook op deze uitzondering wordt hierna ingegaan (zie par. 4.3.3).

3.4 Resumerend: mogelijkheden van zelfregulering binnen het kartelverbod en de uitzonderingen

Het bovenstaande maakt duidelijk dat, ook al is het kartelverbod van toepassing, uitzonderingen kunnen worden ingeroepen. Het hierna volgende hoofdstuk gaat hier verder op in. Er zijn echter ook andere mogelijkheden voor melkveehouders om hun belangen af te wegen tegen de Europese mededingingsbepalingen. Hoofdstuk 4 laat zien dat er ondanks wat hiervoor is vermeld, zelfs mogelijkheden bestaan voor de melkveehouders om in geval van zelfregulering geheel onder het kartelverbod uit te komen:

- Ten eerste gelden specifieke regels voor de landbouwsector: sommige afspraken vallen geheel buiten het mededingingsrecht. Dit is onderwerp van paragraaf 4.1, hierna.
- Ook is er de mogelijkheid van een beroep op de 'uitzondering' voor afspraken die onder een bepaalde omvang blijven. Het gaat om twee mededingingsrechtelijke leerstukken die in elkaars verlengde liggen, merkbaarheid en bagatel, waarop in paragraaf 4.2 verder wordt ingegaan.
- Bovendien geldt dat er wellicht een mogelijkheid is om binnen de verbodsbepaling toch rekening te houden met de belangen die de melkveehouders voorstaan. Hierop wordt in paragraaf 4.3.1 nader ingegaan.

Daarnaast is er aantal *uitzonderingen*, maar uitzonderingen worden per definitie strikt geïnterpreteerd en er zijn maar weinig precedenten die hier als lichtend voorbeeld zouden kunnen dienen. Desalniettemin gaan wij in op:

- de uitzondering van artikel 101 lid 3 VWEU (zie par. 4.3.2);
- de uitzondering voor ondernemingen, belast met diensten van algemeen economisch belang (zie par. 4.3.3).

4 De verhouding tussen landbouwbeleid en mededingingsrecht

In dit hoofdstuk staat de verhouding tussen het landbouwbeleid en de mededinging centraal en wordt ingegaan op de volgende drie vragen:

1. Zijn de mededingingsregels van toepassing op de landbouwsector en meer specifiek op de zuivelsector?

Zo ja:

2. In hoeverre biedt het merkbaarheidsvereiste ruimte voor melkveehouders om tot zelfregulering over te gaan?
3. Of, in hoeverre kan bij de toepassing van de mededingingsregels rekening gehouden worden met het bijzondere karakter van landbouw en/of andere doelstellingen van algemeen belang die verband houden met het landbouwbeleid?

4.1 De verhouding tussen landbouwbeleid en mededingingsrecht

Het uitgangspunt is dat de EU-mededingingsbepalingen in beginsel van toepassing zijn op alle sectoren van de economie. Overigens geldt in het algemeen wat de verhouding tussen het landbouwbeleid en de internemarktbepalingen betreft, en meer in het bijzonder de vrijverkeerregels, dat deze bepalingen als integrerend onderdeel van de gemeenschappelijke marktordeningen worden beschouwd.[1] Artikel 42 VWEU bepaalt evenwel dat de mededingingsregels slechts in de landbouwsector van toepassing zijn, voor zover de Raad dat heeft bepaald met onder meer inachtneming van de doeleinden uit artikel 39 VWEU (zie hiervoor, par. 1.1).

Verordening 1184/2006

Ter uitvoering van artikel 42 VWEU is Verordening 26/62 tot stand gekomen, die inmiddels vervangen is door Verordening 1184/2006.[2] Artikel 1 van deze verordening bepaalt dat

1 Conclusie A-G Mengozzi van 16 september 2010 in zaak C-161/09 (*Kakavetsos-Fragkopoulos (Griekse krentenzaak)*), r.o. 34.

2 Pb. EU L 214 van 4 augustus 2006, p. 7.

artikel 81 tot en met 86 van het EG-Verdrag (nu: art. 101 tot en met 106 VWEU) van toepassing zijn op de voortbrenging van de handel in de in bijlage I van het Verdrag vermelde producten, waaronder melk- en zuivelproducten. De toepasselijkheid geldt echter behoudens het bepaalde in artikel 2 van de verordening. Daarin is bepaald:

> 'Artikel 2
>
> 1. Artikel 81 lid 1, van het Verdrag [nu: art. 101 lid 1 VWEU; *AG & SdV*] is niet van toepassing op de in artikel 1 van deze verordening bedoelde overeenkomsten, besluiten en gedragingen die een wezenlijk bestanddeel uitmaken van een nationale marktorganisatie of die vereist zijn voor de verwezenlijking van de in artikel 33 van het Verdrag [nu: art. 39 VWEU; *AG & SdV*] omschreven doelstellingen.
>
> Het is in het bijzonder niet van toepassing op de overeenkomsten, besluiten en gedragingen van landbouwondernemers, verenigingen van landbouwondernemers of verenigingen van deze verenigingen binnen een lidstaat, voor zover deze, zonder de verplichting in te houden een bepaalde prijs toe te passen, betrekking hebben op de voortbrenging of de verkoop van landbouwproducten of het gebruik van gemeenschappelijke installaties voor het opslaan, behandelen of verwerken van landbouwproducten, tenzij de Commissie vast stelt dat de mededinging zodoende wordt uitgesloten of dat de doeleinden van artikel 33 van het Verdrag [nu: art. 39 VWEU; *AG & SdV*]in gevaar worden gebracht.'

In feite gaat het in artikel 2 om *drie* uitzonderingen op de regel dat de mededingingsregels toepasselijk zijn. Dat zou betekenen dat er voor landbouwers, zoals de melkveehouders, meer ruimte is om met het mededingingsrecht in principe strijdige regelingen toch door te voeren. Let wel op dat op grond van deze Verordening 1184/2006 uitsluitend *de Commissie* bevoegd is om vast te stellen of artikel 101 VWEU kan worden toegepast. De nationale rechter en nationale mededingingsautoriteiten kunnen echter wel artikel 101 VWEU toepassen, indien zij de zekerheid hebben verkregen dat de betrokken afspraken niet onder de uitzondering van artikel 2 van Verordening 1184/2006 vallen.[3] Bovendien werd in de *Milk Marque*-zaak door het Hof vastgesteld dat toetsing van de doelstellingen van artikel 39 VWEU en de plicht om deze doelstellingen van het gemeenschappelijk landbouwbeleid met elkaar te verzoenen, als een bevoegdheid van de nationale mededin-

3 Gev. zaken C-319/93, C-40/04 en C-224/94, *Jur.* 1995, p. I-4471 (*Dijkstra*). Zie ook Rb. Rotterdam 4 december 2001, MEDED 00/933-SIMO en MEDED 00/955-SIMO (*Stichting Saneringsfonds Varkensslachterijen (SSV) en U-Vlees B.V. v. d-g NMa*), ov. 2.4.

gingsautoriteit moet worden beschouwd, analoog aan de bevoegdheid van de gemeenschapsinstellingen.[4]

a Eerste uitzondering van artikel 2 Verordening 1184/2006

In de eerste plaats wanneer overeenkomsten worden gesloten in het kader van een nationale marktorganisatie en er geen gemeenschappelijke marktorganisatie is. Deze uitzondering is niet van belang voor de zuivelsector, aangezien hier sprake is van een gemeenschappelijke marktorganisatie. Zij wordt in dit boek dan ook buiten beschouwing gelaten.

b Tweede uitzondering van artikel 2 Verordening 1184/2006

De tweede uitzonderingsgrond heeft betrekking op de noodzaak om de doelstellingen van artikel 39 VWEU te verwezenlijken. Volgens de rechtspraak van het Hof van Justitie EU is hiervoor het bewijs vereist, 'dat de overeenkomst noodzakelijk is ter bereiking van al deze doelstellingen tezamen'.[5] Dat wil zeggen dat de partijen bij de overeenkomst duidelijk moeten maken dat de overeenkomst vereist zou zijn voor alle doelstellingen van het gemeenschappelijk landbouwbeleid.[6]

Hier is onder andere de *Meldoc*-beschikking relevant.[7] In deze zaak concludeert de Europese Commissie dat de speelruimte die Verordening 804/68 betreffende regels voor een gemeenschappelijke marktordening voor de zuivelsector biedt aan corporaties in de zuivelsector, niet betekent dat zij prijsafspraken mogen maken of importbelemmeringen mogen vaststellen. Dergelijke afspraken zouden te veel afwijken van het interventiesysteem dat de Verordening biedt, waardoor de uitzonderingen van Verordening 26/62 niet van toepassing zijn. Nu het interventiesysteem in de zuivelsector dus mogelijk radicaal verandert, zoals uiteengezet in paragraaf 2.2, wat de speelruimte voor particuliere interventies waarschijnlijk *vergroot*, is het de vraag wat dit betekent voor de toepassing van de uitzondering van Verordening 1184/2006

Het feit dat op EU-niveau, bijvoorbeeld, melkquota worden afgeschaft zal, gezien de *Meldoc*-beschikking, er niet toe mogen leiden dat via particuliere initiatieven dergelijk productiebeperkingen alsnog worden ingevoerd. Daar staat tegenover dat het in *Meldoc* duidelijk importbelemmeringen betrof, die nadelig waren voor de positie van zuivelbedrijven uit andere lidstaten. Wanneer de Europese markt niet opgedeeld wordt, lijkt er meer ruimte te bestaan voor particuliere initiatieven.

4 Zaak C-137/00, *Jur.* 2003, p. I-7975 (*Milk Marque*).
5 Zaak C-399/93, *Jur.* 1995, p. I-04515(*OudeLuttikhuis*), r.o. 25.
6 Zaak 71/74, *Jur.* 1975, p. 00563 (*Frubo*), r.o. 24-27.
7 Beschikking 86/596/EEG, *Meldoc*, Pb. EG L 348 van 10 december 1986, p. 50-65.

c Derde uitzondering van artikel 2 Verordening 1184/2006

Het gaat hier om een uitzondering die geldt voor gedragingen die zich binnen één lidstaat afspelen en betrekking hebben op de voortbrenging of verkoop van landbouwproducten of op het gebruik van gemeenschappelijke installaties voor landbouwproducten. Totdat de Commissie heeft vastgesteld dat door de kartellering de mededinging wordt uitgesloten of de doelstellingen van artikel 39 VWEU in gevaar worden gebracht, wordt de geldigheid van dergelijke gedragingen niet betwist,[8] tenzij het gaat om gedragingen die betrekking hebben op een verplichting een bepaalde prijs toe te passen. Deze uitzonderingsgrond is zeer waarschijnlijk niet van toepassing, aangezien de maatregelen die de melkveehouders voorstaan, juist betrekking hebben op de prijs en de productie.

Dit betekent dat de ruimte voor maatregelen in het kader van de doelstellingen waarschijnlijk wordt beperkt vanwege de gemeenschappelijke marktordening. In hoofdstuk 5 wordt ingegaan op de mogelijkheid om niettemin de ruimte te exploreren, in samenspraak met de Europese Commissie.

4.2 De merkbaarheidsregel

Zoals hiervoor genoemd, kunnen afspraken die in beginsel de mededinging beperken, toch onder het verbod 'uitvallen', indien zij niet merkbaar zijn. Anders dan in paragraaf 4.1 en 4.3 gaat het hier niet om een uitzondering waarbij de mogelijke 'publieke belangen' die met landbouw zijn gemoeid, in geding zijn. Deze uitzondering geldt ongeacht het mogelijk publiekbelangkarakter van landbouw en landbouwproducten.

De merkbaarheidsregel manifesteert zich op twee wijzen: de regel is neergelegd in de *de minimis*-bekendmaking van de Commissie, maar vindt zijn oorsprong in de rechtspraak van het Hof van Justitie EU.

Op de eerste plaats geldt dan het volgende. In de *de minimis*-bekendmaking stelt de Commissie dat als bij horizontale afspraken (dat zijn afspraken tussen ondernemingen in dezelfde fase van de productiekolom, dus tussen de melkveehouderijen onderling, al dan niet via een tussenkantoor) ondernemingen zijn betrokken die niet meer dan 10 procent van de markt bezetten, deze afspraken niet onder het verbod vallen.[9] Dat geldt echter *niet* voor hardcoreafspraken, dus voor quota en prijsafspraken blijft deze ruimte beperkt. Dat levert derhalve weinig ruimte op voor onderlinge samenwerking in de vorm die de Nederlandse melkveehouders voorstaan. Bovendien komt een nuttige regulering van de

---

8 Gev. zaken C-319/93, C-40/04 en C-224/94, *Jur.* 1995, p. I-4471 (*Dijkstra*), r.o. 17-18.
9 *De minimis*-bekendmaking, Pb. EU C 368 van 22 december 2001, p. 13-15.

markt alleen tot stand als er juist veel meer dan 10 procent van de markt (de boeren) is betrokken bij de regeling. De algemene regeling opknippen in regionale regelingen helpt, als dat al praktisch uitvoerbaar zou zijn, ook niet: de regelingen worden dan bij elkaar opgeteld.[10]

De *de minimis*-bekendmaking van de Commissie is een *uitwerking* van het leerstuk van merkbaarheid, dat door het Hof van Justitie is ontwikkeld.[11] Volgens de rechtspraak van het Hof geldt ook los van de precieze drempels – ook voor het nationale recht – een zogenoemde merkbaarheidseis: als de impact van de overeenkomst verwaarloosbaar klein is, dan is het verbod niet van toepassing. De marktaandelendrempels in de *de minimis*-bekendmaking zijn in zekere zin een kwantificering van dit leerstuk. Het leerstuk heeft ook een kwalitatieve kant, hoewel dat meer omstreden is. Dat komt hierna terug in de proportionaliteitstoets (zie par. 4.3).[12]

De mogelijkheden voor de melkveehouders om bij afspraken over quota en prijzen in het kader van de merkbaarheidseis onder het kartelverbod uit te komen, zijn dus uitermate gering. Er zal al snel een interstatelijk effect zijn, gezien de ruime interpretatie die het Hof geeft aan het feit dat een overeenkomst de handel tussen lidstaten ongunstig kan beïnvloeden,[13] en het gaat vooral om hardcorebeperkingen, die in ieder geval onder het kartelverbod vallen.

4.3 Rekening houden met doelstellingen landbouwbeleid/zuivelsector binnen de mededingingsregels

Indien de mededingingsregels van toepassing zijn en de regeling is niet zo minimaal dat zij om merkbaarheidsredenen onder het verbod 'uitvalt', dan moet worden bezien wat de ruimte is binnen *het verbod* zelf, of binnen *de uitzondering*, daarmee rekening houdend met de belangen en doelstellingen van de landbouwsector. Zoals in paragrafen 2.1 en 3.1 immers al is vermeld, de Verdragsrechtelijke context is, onder andere via de integratiebepalingen betreffende milieu en dierenwelzijn, relevant voor het landbouw- en mededingingsbeleid.

---

10 Zaak C-234/89, *Jur.* p. I-00935 (*Delimitis*).

11 Zaak 5/69, *Jur.* 1969, p. 295 (*Völk v. Vervaeke*).

12 In de Nederlandse Mededingingswet is een specifieke bagateluitzondering gecreëerd op het verbod in art. 7 lid 2 Mw, die wel van toepassing is op hardcorebeperkingen. Uit art. 7 lid 2 Mw blijkt dat het verbod niet geldt – bij horizontale regelingen – indien voldaan is aan twee cumulatieve voorwaarden: het gezamenlijke marktaandeel van de betrokken ondernemingen bedraagt *ten hoogste 5 procent* op de relevante markt, en de gezamenlijke omzet van de betrokken ondernemingen is niet hoger dan *€ 40.000.000*.

13 Sinds het arrest *Grundig en Consten*, gev. zaken 56 en 58/64, *Jur.* 1966, p. 299.

Het afwegen van 'niet-economische' of publieke belangen tegen beperkingen op de mededinging in het kader van het EU-mededingingsbeleid staat niet alleen sinds een aantal jaren in het hart van de belangstelling, maar is ook vereist op grond van de eerder genoemde integratiebepalingen in het Verdrag (zie par. 2.1).[14]

Drie mogelijkheden komen aan bod, waarbij steeds eerst in het algemeen nader op de mogelijkheid wordt ingegaan, en vervolgens wordt bekeken wat dit de melkveehouders *in concreto* biedt.

4.3.1 Artikel 101 lid 1 VWEU en de leer van de inherente beperking

Inherente beperkingen en belangen van niet-economische aard
Als we kijken naar de wijze waarop de Europese Commissie overeenkomsten toetst aan het kartelverbod, dan zien we dat in een aantal zaken rekening is gehouden met zogenoemde niet-economische belangen, zoals de bescherming van het milieu, de volksgezondheid of cultuur. Gezien de brede werking van het kartelverbod uit artikel 101 lid 1 VWEU (zie hiervoor) kunnen slechts in beperkte mate overwegingen van niet-economische aard worden meegenomen bij de toepassing van artikel 101 lid 1 VWEU. Dit is in het bijzonder het geval in het kader van de zogenoemde leer van de inherente beperkingen.

Bij de leer van de inherente beperkingen gaat het om mededingingsbeperkingen die noodzakelijk worden geacht voor het goed functioneren van een organisatie of sector en daarom buiten het kartelverbod van artikel 101 lid 1 VWEU vallen.[15] Een mooi voorbeeld is de zaak *Gøttrup-Klim*, die overigens de landbouwsector betreft. Het ging hier om bepalingen opgenomen in de statuten van een inkoopcoöperatie, krachtens welke het verboden was voor de participerende bedrijven om deel te nemen aan andere georganiseerde samenwerkingsverbanden die haar rechtstreeks beconcurreerden. Volgens het Hof van Justitie ontsnappen dergelijke beperkingen aan het verbod van artikel 101 lid 1 VWEU, indien 'zij beperkt zijn tot hetgeen noodzakelijk is om de goede werking van de coöperatie te verzekeren en haar contractuele onderhandelingspositie ten opzichte van de producenten te handhaven'.[16]

14 Zie, onder andere: J.W. van de Gronden & K.J.M. Mortelmans, *Mededinging en niet-economische belangen*, Deventer: Kluwer 2001; S.A. de Vries 2006 (zie noot 6 van hoofdstuk 2); H. Vedder, *Competition Law and Environmental Protection in Europa; Towards Sustainability?*, Groningen: Europa Law Publishing 2003; C. Townley, *Article 81 EC and Public Policy*, Oxford and Portland: Hart Publishing, 2009.

15 J. Houdijk, *Publieke belangen in het mededingingsrecht: een onderzoek in vijf domeinen*, Deventer: Kluwer, 2009, p. 671.

16 Zaak C-250/92, *Jur.* 1994, p. I-05641 (*Gottrup-Klim*), r.o. 35.

In de *Wouters*-zaak werd de leer van de inherente beperking toegepast op een andere sector en verder uitgewerkt en uitgebreid.[17] Het Hof bepaalde namelijk dat deontologische regels, zoals in deze zaak het verbod voor advocaten, ingesteld door de Nederlandse Orde van Advocaten, om een geïntegreerd samenwerkingsverband aan te gaan met accountants ter bescherming van de onafhankelijkheid van de advocatuur, een gerechtvaardigde beperking op het kartelverbod vormen. Of *alle* publieke belangen van deze benadering kunnen profiteren, lijkt af te hangen van de economische en juridische context waarbinnen het besluit is genomen.

Uit een andere uitspraak van het Hof op het gebied van sport, de *Meca-Medina*-zaak, blijkt dat een antidopingregeling (en de daaruit voortvloeiende sancties), die opgesteld was door de Olympische zwembond, mededingingsbeperkingen met zich mee kan brengen, maar dat deze beperkingen niet verdergaan dan noodzakelijk en proportioneel zijn om de legitieme doelstellingen (integriteit van de competitie en de gezondheid van de sporters te behouden c.q. regelmatig verloop van de wedstrijden) te verzekeren.[18] In deze benadering kan aan de hand van een proportionaliteitstoets beoordeeld worden of bepaalde publieke belangen, ondanks eventuele in het geding zijnde mededingingsbeperkingen, toch gerechtvaardigd zijn in het licht van het kartelverbod. In de zaken *Meca-Medina* en *Wouters* heeft het Hof in feite een rechtstreekse afweging van mededingings- en publieke belangen gemaakt, die de leer van de inherente beperking overstijgt.[19]

De vraag die dan vervolgens rijst, is welke mededingingsbeperkingen als noodzakelijk en evenredig kunnen worden beschouwd binnen de context van het kartelverbod. Prijsafspraken, quota en marktverdelingsafspraken worden vaak als hardcorebeperkingen gezien en lijken daarom moeilijk te rechtvaardigen. Maar wanneer de prijs slechts een 'component' of een factor is van een aantal kostenfactoren van een bepaalde activiteit of dienst, dan valt de overeenkomst mogelijk buiten het kartelverbod. Volgens het Hof in de *Pavlov*-zaak beperkt de overeenkomst de mededinging in dat geval niet merkbaar. In deze zaak ging het om de kosten van een aanvullende pensioenregeling voor medisch specialisten, waarop de artsen elkaar weliswaar niet beconcurreren, maar die slechts van marginale invloed zijn op de totale kosten van de door medisch specialisten aangeboden diensten.[20] Daarbij is wel van belang dat het Hof meewoog dat de prijscomponent in de *Pavlov*-zaak uiteindelijk weinig impact had op de prijs die de consument op de markt betaalt.

---

17 Zaak C-309/99, *Jur.* 2002, p. I-1577 (*Wouters*).
18 Zaak C-519/04 P, *Jur.* 2006, p. I-06991 (*Meca-Medina*).
19 Zie ook Townley 2009, p. 132-133 (zie noot 14 van dit hoofdstuk).
20 Zaak C-180/98 t/m C-184/98, *Jur.* 2000, p. I-06451 (*Pavlov*), r.o. 95.

Ook al lijkt de leer van de inherente beperking de mogelijkheden te verruimen om publieke belangen na te streven door particuliere initiatieven binnen de context van artikel 101 lid 1 VWEU, is voorzichtigheid hier toch geboden.[21] Het Hof heeft deze leer (nog) op lang niet alle sectoren toegepast. Dat echter steeds vaker rekening moet worden gehouden met de specifieke eigenschappen van een bepaalde sector, lijkt buiten twijfel te staan[22] en dit wordt versterkt door de centrale plaats die de integratiebepaling nu in het EU-Werkingsverdrag inneemt (zie hiervoor, par. 2.1).

Toepassing op de melksector

De vraag is in hoeverre specifieke, aan de zuivelsector gerelateerde belangen, meegenomen kunnen en moeten worden bij de toepassing van de mededingingsregels. Uit het voorgaande volgt dat de landbouwsector nog steeds als een bijzondere sector wordt beschouwd, waarop weliswaar de mededingingsregels van toepassing zijn, maar waarbij ook rekening gehouden moet worden met de doelstellingen van landbouwbeleid.

Bij de toepassing van het kartelverbod van artikel 101 lid 1 VWEU zou beargumenteerd kunnen worden dat sommige mededingingsbeperkingen noodzakelijk zijn om doelstellingen die inherent zijn aan de landbouwsector, te kunnen realiseren. Gezien de bijzondere aard van deze sector en het feit dat de doelstellingen ook expliciet in het EU-Werkingsverdrag zijn opgenomen, hoeven mededingingsbeperkende overeenkomsten niet zonder meer onder het kartelverbod van artikel 101 lid 1 VWEU te vallen. In het licht van de *Meca-Medina*-uitspraak hangt een en ander af van de noodzakelijkheid en evenredigheid van de afspraken voor de beoordeling in hoeverre dergelijke overeenkomsten toch te rechtvaardigen zijn vanwege bepaalde doelstellingen van, bijvoorbeeld, voedselvoorziening, natuurbehoud, of andere aan het landbouwbeleid gerelateerde publieke doelstellingen. En gezien de brede benadering van het Hof in *Wouters* en *Meca-Medina* is het niet ondenkbeeldig dat dergelijke doelstellingen worden afgewogen tegen de beperking die het verwezenlijken van de doelstellingen met zich brengt voor de mededinging.

De grens ligt in ieder geval bij het opnemen van bepaalde hardcorerestricties, zoals het vaststellen van quota en prijzen, tenzij de prijs slechts een component vormt van de totale kosten van melkveehouders (*Pavlov*-zaak). Een dergelijk 'merkbaarheidspleidooi' zou met enige moeite kunnen worden opgezet voor een heffing ten bate van een melkfonds. Als de heffing (per eenheid melk) zo minimaal is dat hij geen of vrijwel geen uitwerking heeft op de door de consument te betalen prijs, zou deze redenering kunnen worden gebruikt. De valkuil is het criterium van de minimale invloed op de prijs: niet alleen is er maar één

21 Houdijk 2009, p. 97 (zie noot 48).

22 Zie ook zaak T-168/01, *Jur.* 2006, p. II-02969 (*GlaxoSmithKline*), r.o. 122-147.

voorbeeld bekend waarin het merkbaarheidsleerstuk op deze wijze is toegepast, ook zal niet snel worden aangenomen dat die invloed minimaal is. Bovendien, indien de bedoeling is om uit de heffing een fonds te financieren dat in tijden van overaanbod het aanbod uit de markt moet halen (via een interventie), dan kan ook dat worden gezien als productiebeperking. De heffing ten bate van het melkfonds is slechts een onderdeel van het geheel van de regeling. Hoewel, anders dus dan bij de *de minimis*-drempel, er niet zozeer een beperking is van de grootte van de groep die mag meedoen aan een regeling, biedt ook deze kwalitatieve merkbaarheid uiteindelijk een lastige kapstok.

Hiervoor is wel opgemerkt dat de leer van de inherente beperking nog in ontwikkeling is en het vooralsnog onduidelijk is in hoeverre deze leer door de mededingingsautoriteiten zal worden gevolgd op het terrein van landbouw.

4.3.2 De exceptie van artikel 101 lid 3 VWEU en 'niet-economische' belangen

Aangezien artikel 101 lid 3 VWEU niet verwijst naar publieke belangen, is het de vraag in hoeverre daar bij de toepassing van deze bepaling überhaupt wel rekening mee kan worden gehouden. Eén interpretatie van artikel 101 lid 3 VWEU is dan ook dat deze bepaling slechts een afweging vormt tussen de mededingingsbeperkende effecten van een gedraging en de vergroting van economische doelmatigheid.[23] Een dergelijke interpretatie zou de mogelijkheid om rekening te houden met algemene belangen, zoals milieueffecten, beperken. Een andere is echter dat artikel 101 lid 3 VWEU uitgaat van een breder welvaartsbegrip, dat ook rekening houdt met de voordelen van een afspraak die verband houden met het welzijn van de consument.[24] Daarnaast kan wederom gewezen worden op de integratiebepalingen die in het Verdrag zijn opgenomen en die de Europese Instellingen verplichten om in het vormgeven en uitvoeren van beleid en regelgeving rekening te houden met verschillende publieke belangen, zoals artikel 11 VWEU voor het milieubelang, artikel 13 VWEU voor dierenwelzijn en zelfs wellicht artikel 167 lid 4 VWEU voor culturele aspecten.[25]

Er bestaat inderdaad een tendens om meer rekening te houden met publieke belangen, die het meest duidelijk is op het terrein van het milieu.[26] Uit de CECED-beschikking van de Europese Commissie blijken ook gunstige effecten van een overeenkomst voor de gehele samenleving en niet alleen voor individuele consumenten binnen de reikwijdte van artikel

23 Zie, bijvoorbeeld, R. Whish, *Competition Law*, London: Butterworths, 2001, p. 125-128.
24 G. Monti, 'Article 81 EC and Public Policy', *Common Market Law Review* 2002, p. 1065.
25 Zie ook De Vries 2006 (zie noot 6 van hoofdstuk 2).
26 Zie, bijvoorbeeld, Vedder 2003 (zie noot 14 van dit hoofdstuk).

101 lid 3 VWEU te kunnen vallen. Bij mededingingsbeperkende overeenkomsten die milieudoelstellingen beogen te realiseren, zijn door de Commissie milieuvoordelen als rechtstreekse voordelen voor de consument beschouwd.[27]

Bij de toepassing van de proportionaliteitstoets wordt het consumentenbelang niet vaak als een apart onderscheidend belang gezien, maar meegenomen als onderdeel van de gunstige economische effecten van de samenwerking. Bovendien laten milieuzaken zien dat kostenreductie voor consumenten niet altijd als noodzakelijk onderdeel van de proportionaliteitstoets wordt beschouwd; de verbetering van de milieukwaliteit kan ook als gunstig voor consumenten worden gezien, ook al leidt dit op korte termijn tot prijsverhogingen. Het belang van het proportionaliteitsbeginsel is groot. Aan de hand van dit beginsel wordt bekeken of de beperkingen op de mededinging uiteindelijk gerechtvaardigd zijn.

Twee andere relevante voorbeelden – maar ook al wat oudere, zodat de relevantie daarvan in het huidige tijdsgewricht met voorbehoud moet worden beoordeeld – van de toepassing van de voorwaarden van artikel 101 lid 3 VWEU geven de *Ford/Volkswagen*-beschikking en de *Baksteen*-beschikking van de Commissie. In de eerste beschikking woog de Commissie het creëren van banen en het aantrekken van investeerders mee in het vaststellen dat de voorwaarden van artikel 101 lid 3 waren vervuld.[28] Het ging daarbij om het oprichten van een autofabriek in een van de (destijds) armste delen van Europa, namelijk Portugal, waarbij rechtstreeks vijfduizend banen zouden worden gecreëerd, en meer indirect wellicht nog eens tienduizend banen. Daarnaast zouden door de oprichting van deze autofabriek andere investeringen worden aangetrokken. Alle andere voorwaarden van artikel 101 lid 3 VWEU waren verder (ook) vervuld, maar deze overweging speelde zeker een rol bij de beoordeling.

In het voorbeeld van de *Baksteen*-beschikking geldt dat de Commissie vaststelde dat aan de voorwaarden van artikel 101 lid 3 VWEU was voldaan, ondanks het feit dat de overeenkomst tussen baksteenfabrikanten een productiebeperking inhield. Een productiebeperking wordt normaal gesproken als zeer ernstig voor de mededinging aangemerkt. Deze productiebeperking werd echter afgesproken als onderdeel van saneringsmaatregelen, waarbij overcapaciteit – definitief – uit de markt zou worden gehaald. De Commissie hield er daarbij rekening mee dat door deze afspraken de herstructurering onder sociaal acceptabele

---

27 Beschikking 2000/475 (*CECED*), Pb. EU 2000, L 187/47; Beschikking 94/332 (*Exxon/Shell*), Pb. EU 1994, L 144/20.

28 Ook dit was onder het oude systeem, waarbij art. 81 lid 3 EG (nu art. 101 lid 3 VWEU) nog geen rechtstreekse werking had (zoals nu het geval is), en er nog een ontheffing moest worden gevraagd. Daarom heeft de Commissie zich hierover in een beschikking uitgelaten: zie Beschikking van de *Commissie Ford/Volkswagen*, Pb. EU 1993, L 20/14.

omstandigheden (gefaseerd, geordend) zou plaatshebben in plaats van door veel disruptievere plotselinge faillissementen.[29]

Niettemin is het beleid van de Europese Commissie op het terrein van publieke belangen en mededingingsbeleid nog niet uitgekristalliseerd. Uit randnummer 42 van de richtsnoeren betreffende de toepassing van artikel 81 lid 3 EG (nu: artikel 101 lid 3 VWEU) blijkt dat de Commissie dan ook een meer voorzichtige benadering voorstaat bij de toetsing van andere, publieke, belangen aan artikel 101 lid 3: 'Doelstellingen die worden nagestreefd met andere Verdragsbepalingen kunnen in aanmerking worden genomen in zoverre zij onder de vier voorwaarden van artikel 101 lid 3, kunnen worden begrepen.'[30]

Melkveehouders

Artikel 101 lid 3 EG lijkt dus ruimte te bieden voor het nastreven van publieke belangen door ondernemingen, zoals de Nederlandse (en Europese) melkveehouders. Hiervoor is geconstateerd dat binnen de context van artikel 101 lid 3 VWEU, ook op lange termijn, rekening gehouden kan worden met milieuvoordelen die de gehele samenleving ten goede komen. Voor de Nederlandse (en Europese) melkveehouders is dit van belang, niet in de laatste plaats vanwege de rol die melkveehouders spelen in natuurbehoud, landschapsontwikkeling en de verbetering van het milieu. Daarbij kan ook gedacht worden aan het principe dat producten die dicht bij huis worden geproduceerd, de minste impact hebben – uitgedrukt als kleine ecologische voetstap – in vergelijking met producten die van ver worden gehaald; het is voor ons echter moeilijk in te schatten of een dergelijke redenering daadwerkelijk opgaat, gezien productiemethoden en transportkosten. Ook voedselveiligheid kan hier een rol spelen. Indien de melkveehouders afspraken maken die een duidelijke bijdrage leveren aan het verwezenlijken van deze doelstellingen, zou een beroep op artikel 101 lid 3 VWEU in beginsel openstaan.

Wanneer zelfregulering ook beoogt te vermijden dat zich sociaal onacceptabele toestanden op de markt voordoen en beoogt overcapaciteit tegen te gaan, wat noodzakelijk zou zijn vanwege de specifieke concurrentiekenmerken van de markt voor melk, en daarnaast bijdraagt aan de bestaansvoorwaarden van de melkveehouderij op langere termijn, is een betoog gebaseerd op artikel 101 lid 3 VWEU steviger. Waar milieudoelstellingen echter steeds meer geaccepteerd zijn, is dat voor de meer 'sociale aspecten' van beperkende regelingen nog een openstaande vraag.

---

29 Beschikking *Stichting Baksteen*, Pb. EU 1994, L 131/15. Zie ook *Synthetische vezels*-beschikking, Pb. EG 1984, L 207/17.

30 Bekendmaking Commissie toepassing art. 81 lid 3 EG, Pb. EU C 101, 27 april 2004, p. 97-118.

Overigens heeft het Hof van Justitie EU al eerder bepaald dat een langetermijndoelstelling essentieel kan zijn voor het inroepen van een rechtvaardigingsgrond. In de *Romkes*- en *Kramer*-zaken stelde het Hof dat nationale maatregelen tot beperking van de visserij geen maatregelen van gelijke werking als kwantitatieve invoerbeperkingen in de zin van artikel 34 VWEU (vrij verkeer van goederen) zijn, op grond van het feit dat die maatregelen, hoewel op korte termijn leidend tot een vermindering van de hoeveelheden vis die tussen de lidstaten kunnen worden verhandeld, bedoeld zijn om op lange termijn een optimale opbrengst van de visserij te verzekeren.[31] Hierbij moet wel opgemerkt worden dat het in *Romkes* en *Kramer* ging om *overheidsmaatregelen* die getoetst werden aan, onder andere, artikel 34 VWEU, dat een grotere ruimte biedt dan artikel 101 VWEU om productiebeperkingen te rechtvaardigen. Publieke belangen worden immers in de eerste plaats door de overheid gewaarborgd.[32]

Niet alleen op het terrein van het milieu, maar ook op andere terreinen, zoals gezondheidszorg en, bijvoorbeeld, cultuur, wordt in meerdere of mindere mate rekening gehouden met publieke belangen. Niettemin moeten, in tegenstelling tot de leer van de inherente beperking, de *vier* voorwaarden van artikel 101 lid 3 VWEU zijn vervuld voordat door de melkveehouders een geslaagd beroep op deze uitzondering kan worden gedaan. Dit kan een probleem zijn, aangezien het instrument van zelfregulering, beoogd door de melkveehouders, wel noodzakelijk moet zijn om de doelstellingen te bereiken en niet verder mag gaan dan daarvoor nodig is. Veel hangt dan af van de precieze vormgeving van de regeling en de doelstellingen die daarmee (daadwerkelijk!) worden geprobeerd te bewerkstelligen.

4.3.3 Diensten van algemeen economisch belang van artikel 106 lid 2 VWEU

Artikel 106 lid 2 VWEU bevat een specifieke uitzondering voor ondernemingen die belast zijn met taken van algemeen economisch belang en is niet alleen van belang voor artikel 106 lid 1 VWEU, maar ook voor andere bepalingen uit het EU-Werkingsverdrag, zoals, bijvoorbeeld, het verbod op staatssteun of het kartelverbod. Om een beroep op artikel 106 lid 2 VWEU te doen, moet de desbetreffende onderneming wel met een taak van algemeen economisch belang zijn belast en deze taak moet duidelijk omgeschreven zijn in nationale regelgeving. Het uitgangspunt bij de definitie en toewijzing van taken van algemeen economisch belang is volgens vaste jurisprudentie dat de lidstaten over een ruime discretionaire bevoegdheid beschikken en dat de Commissie slechts toetst op kennelijke fouten.[33] Deze ruime bevoegdheid van de lidstaten is (deels) verklaarbaar doordat een definitie van

---

31 Zaak 46/86, *Jur.* 1987, p. 02671 (*Romkes*), r.o. 24 en gev. zaken 3, 4 en 6/76, *Jur.* 1976, p. 01279 (*Kramer*).
32 De Vries 2006, p. 337 (zie noot 6 van hoofdstuk 2).
33 Zaak T-289/03, *Jur.* 2008, p. II-00081(*BUPA/Commissie*).

diensten van algemeen economisch belang in het EU-Verdrag en EU-Werkingsverdrag ontbreekt, artikel 14 VWEU het belang van deze diensten onderstreept en dat op een aantal terreinen, zoals de gezondheidszorg en woningbouw, de lidstaten primair bevoegd zijn om maatregelen te nemen. Maar ook op andere terreinen, zoals milieu, waar de lidstaten en de Gemeenschap hun bevoegdheid delen, hebben lidstaten een ruime discretionaire bevoegdheid om diensten van algemeen economisch belang te definiëren en toe te kennen.

Melkveehouders

Deze laatste mogelijkheid om aan het kartelverbod te ontsnappen, is alleen van belang voor ondernemingen die *door de lidstaat* zijn belast met een taak van algemeen economisch belang. Wanneer de melkveehouders in toenemende mate worden geconfronteerd met taken, verplichtingen die de natuur en het milieu betreffen, zoals natuurbehoud en landschapsbeheer, dan zouden zij de overheid moeten vragen om op een expliciete wijze, dat wil zeggen door middel van regelgeving, met deze taken te worden belast. In dat geval staat een beroep op artikel 106 lid 2 VWEU open met alle voordelen van dien. De proportionaliteitstoets, zoals hiervoor kort uiteengezet, wordt op een 'mildere' wijze uitgevoerd dan in het kader van artikel 101 lid 3 VWEU. Maar dan zullen melkveehouders bij de nationale overheid moeten bewerkstelligen een dergelijke taak opgelegd te krijgen. Het probleem met deze route is wel dat hardcorebeperkingen zelden deze proportionaliteitstoets zullen kunnen doorstaan.

5 Mogelijkheden om het landbouw- en mededingingsbeleid aan te passen

Uit het voorgaande blijkt dat er weliswaar ruimte bestaat voor zelfregulering binnen de context van de mededingingsregels, maar dat deze vooralsnog beperkt is. In dit hoofdstuk zal dan ook bekeken worden of er geen mogelijkheden zijn op basis van het Europese recht om rechtsinstrumenten te creëren die de belangen van de melkveehouders in Nederland en Europa beter waarborgen.

5.1 Landbouwbeleid

Het landbouwbeleid behoort weliswaar volgens het EU-Verdrag tot de gedeelde bevoegdheden van de Europese Unie en de lidstaten, maar de Europese wetgever heeft veelvuldig gebruikgemaakt van deze bevoegdheid, zodat de lidstaten slechts taken van 'medebewind' uitvoeren. Voor de melkveehouders betekent dit dat het EU-beleid moet worden beïnvloed, eventueel via nationale kanalen, aangezien het landbouwbeleid grotendeels nationaal wordt voorbereid, met het oog op, bijvoorbeeld, het afschaffen van quota. Dit is echter, gezien de plannen van de Europese Commissie, geen realistische optie.

Een andere optie is de totstandkoming van een Europees kader, waarin de door de melkveehouders beoogde zelfregulering een kader wordt gegeven. Op EU-niveau zelf worden al voorwaarden geschapen – de bevoegdheid – voor een interventiesysteem *á la Canadienne*. Dit zou betekenen dat een regeling door de melkveehouders een rechtsgrond krijgt. Het politieke klimaat lijkt nu het momentum te kunnen bieden voor het zich beijveren voor een dergelijk kader. Zo is de 'Groep op hoog niveau' (*High Level Group on Milk*) in haar rapport van 15 juni 2010 van oordeel dat

> 'het bewustzijn en de verantwoordelijkheid van de marktdeelnemers in de zuivelketen moet worden versterkt teneinde meer rekening te houden met de signalen van de markt en het aanbod af te stemmen op de vraag. De deskundigengroep verzoekt de Commissie dan ook zich te beraden over het meest passende middel (richtsnoeren of wetgevingsvoorstel) om het vrijwillige gebruik van formele, schriftelijke, vooraf opgestelde contracten voor de levering van rauwe melk te bevorderen.'

Essentiële aspecten van dit contract zou de te betalen prijs en hoeveelheid van levering zijn.

In de Raadszitting van 27 september 2010 betreffende landbouw en visserij blijkt een ruime meerderheid van de lidstaten (22) de conclusies van de 'Groep op hoog niveau' te steunen en de Commissie op te roepen te reageren, met name op de volgende drie aanbevelingen van deze groep:

- betere contractuele voorwaarden tussen melkproducenten en zuivelfabrieken;
- de collectieve onderhandelingsmacht van de producenten; en
- de mogelijke rol van brancheorganisaties in de zuivelsector.

Bij de afronding van dit boek heeft de Commissie inderdaad een voorstel gepresenteerd in reactie op de aanbevelingen van de 'Groep op hoog niveau'. Van belang is daarbij ook dat sinds het Verdrag van Lissabon het Europees Parlement een actieve rol in de besluitvorming heeft gekregen en dat kan worden aangesproken om de belangen van de melkveehouders te bevorderen (zie ook par. 2.1).[1]

5.2 Landbouwbeleid en mededingingsrecht

Niet alleen het landbouwbeleid in zijn geheel, maar ook de toepassing van de tweede uitzondering van artikel 2 Verordening 1184/2006 kan uitkomst bieden. Deze heeft, zoals gezegd, betrekking op de noodzaak om de doelstellingen van artikel 39 VWEU te verwezenlijken. Het gaat er dan om dat vanuit de visie van de melkveehouders de overeenkomst vereist zou zijn voor alle doelstellingen van het gemeenschappelijk landbouwbeleid. Nu het landbouwbeleid bestaat uit drie componenten (de politiek-economische component, waarbij landbouw bijdraagt aan de economische groei; de sociaal-politieke component, waaronder zorg voor de plattelandspopulatie, waaronder een stabiel inkomen, en het plattelandsbeleid (*rural development*), dat meer recent een nieuwe impuls heeft gekregen; de sociaaleconomische component, die de voedselvoorziening van consumenten betreft, zie par. 2.1 hiervoor).

Daarbij moet het niet alleen gaan om een stabiel inkomen, maar de voorgenomen zelfregulering moet ook daadwerkelijk bijdragen aan plattelandsbeleid – argumenten daartoe liggen in het verlengde van stabiele inkomens, maar gaan verder dan dat – en veilige voedselvoorziening. Daartoe zou bijvoorbeeld gedacht kunnen worden aan kwaliteitseisen. Die kwaliteitseisen mogen echter weer niet mededingingsbeperkend zijn.

1 Zie ook Press Release (provisional version) of the 3042nd Council Meeting of 26 October 2010, te vinden op: <www.consilium.europa.eu/uedocs/cms_data/docs/pressdata/en/agricult/117419.pdf>.

Ook de aanbevelingen van de 'Groep op hoog niveau' hebben betrekking op kwaliteitsnormen en innovatie in het gemeenschappelijk landbouwbeleid, met name in het plattelandontwikkelingsbeleid. De zuivelsector wordt uitgenodigd om zelf mee te denken over het concurrentievermogen van de voedselketen.

5.3 Een mededingingsrechtelijke interpretatie van de Europese Commissie?

De Europese Commissie heeft de bevoegdheid om een oordeel te geven over overeenkomsten of regelingen die van groot belang zijn, bijvoorbeeld omdat zij een nieuwe rechtsvraag betreffen. Om te voorkomen dat de hervormingen die Verordening 1/2003 met zich brengt, juist teniet worden gedaan door het toestaan van al te ruimhartige mogelijkheden om de Commissie te bevragen, heeft zij in een mededeling nadere voorwaarden opgesteld.[2] Onder punt 8 van de mededeling staat het volgende:

> 'Onder het voorbehoud van punt 7 zal de Commissie, wanneer bij haar een verzoek om een adviesbrief wordt ingediend, nagaan of dit verzoek in behandeling kan worden genomen. Het opstellen van een adviesbrief kan alleen worden overwogen indien aan alle volgende voorwaarden is voldaan:
>
> a. De inhoudelijke toetsing van een overeenkomst of gedraging aan de artikelen 81 en/of 82 van het Verdrag doet een vraag rijzen inzake de toepassing van het recht waarop geen antwoord gegeven wordt in het bestaande regelgevingskader van de EG, met inbegrip van de jurisprudentie van de communautaire rechterlijke instanties, en evenmin in openbaar toegankelijke algemene richtsnoeren of in een precedent uit de beschikkingenpraktijk of in eerdere adviesbrieven.
> b. Op grond van een eerste beoordeling van de specifieke omstandigheden en de achtergrond van het geval lijkt het nuttig via een adviesbrief opheldering over de nieuwe vraag te verschaffen, rekening houdend met de volgende elementen:
>   - het economische belang vanuit het gezichtspunt van de verbruiker van de goederen of diensten waarop de overeenkomst of de gedraging betrekking heeft, en/of
>   - de mate waarin de overeenkomst of de gedraging overeenkomt met of waarschijnlijk zal overeenkomen met een wijder verbreid economisch gebruik op de markt en/of

2 Mededeling van de Commissie over informeel advies betreffende nieuwe vragen met betrekking tot art. 1 en 82 van het EG-Verdrag die in individuele gevallen rijzen (adviesbrieven), Pb. EU 2004, C 101/78.

- de omvang van de investeringen die met de transactie gemoeid zijn in relatie tot de grootte van de betrokken ondernemingen en de mate waarin de transactie verband houdt met een structurele operatie, zoals de oprichting van een niet volwaardige gemeenschappelijke onderneming.

c. Het is mogelijk dat een adviesbrief wordt opgesteld op basis van de verstrekte informatie, zonder dat er dus verder feitelijk onderzoek nodig is.'

Bij het directoraat-generaal Mededinging van de Commissie kan aan de hand van een uitgewerkt plan de vraag worden voorgelegd of een door de melkveehouders beoogde regeling, onder de 'leer van inherente beperkingen' zou kunnen worden geaccepteerd; over de vraag of de regeling wellicht onder de *Pavlov*-formule kan worden gevrijwaard van het verbod; of dat zij kan worden geschaard onder de exceptie van artikel 101 lid 3 VWEU. Het hiervoor uiteengezette kader van mededingingsrecht laat wel zien dat de ruimte beperkt is: de regeling zou zich zo weinig mogelijk moeten richten op daadwerkelijke ingrepen in prijs en productie, en zo veel mogelijk op het belang dat is gediend met landbouw en de melksector als geheel. Daarom ligt een prijsregeling gevoelig; een opkoopregeling bij overproductie eveneens.

Bovendien heeft een dergelijke regeling vooral zijn nut als het een Europa-brede regeling betreft. Een regeling die zich richt op een individuele lidstaat, bijvoorbeeld Nederland of Frankrijk, kan wel nuttig zijn vanuit nationaal perspectief, maar heeft als gevolg – als de Nederlandse boeren als enige een heffing op hun melkprijs krijgen – dat zij zichzelf uit de Europese markt kunnen prijzen. Dat standpunt is van belang, omdat zelfs bij een nationale regeling de *Europese* mededingingsregels (ook) van toepassing zullen zijn: een regeling waarbij het merendeel van de melkveehouders in Nederland is aangesloten, heeft namelijk ook een effect op de interstatelijke handel. Overigens blijkt dat de reden voor prijsafspraken tussen melkveehouders en leveranciers van melkproducten in Frankrijk het inkomensbehoud is voor de Franse melksector in tijden van grote concurrentie van de Duitse melksector. Dit maakt een Europese aanpak des te dringender.

De 'Groep op hoog niveau' stelt voor dat tussen melkveehouders en melkverwerkers afspraken gemaakt worden over prijzen en hoeveelheid – verticale afspraken – teneinde beter rekening te houden met de signalen van de markt en het aanbod af te stemmen op de vraag. Dit lijkt ook het doel van de Franse regeling.

Vanuit mededingingsrechtelijk perspectief zou het creëren van een fonds, bestaande uit een kleine heffing op de melkproductie, een alternatief vormen. Die creatie draagt een zekere prijsbinding in zich, wat mededingingsrechtelijk in algemene zin lastig is te verkopen. Als het fonds zich beperkt tot een miniem deel van de prijs, waardoor het effect op de

consumentenprijs nihil is, kan worden beargumenteerd dat de mededingingsinvloed niet merkbaar is (via de *Pavlov*-route). Wat de oprichting van een fonds en productiebeperkingen in het algemeen betreft, is van belang om te onderbouwen welke doelen met dergelijke regelingen nu precies worden nagestreefd. Met een fonds en quota staat het belang centraal van het voorkomen van overproductie en het stabiliseren van de markt, wat op lange termijn ten dienste staat aan het in stand houden van het platteland, ecologisch beheer, goede kwaliteit van de voedselvoorziening en dergelijke. Hoe draagt de regeling die de melkveehouders voorstaan, bij aan deze doelen van algemeen belang? Benadrukt dient te worden dat hoe meer het algemeen belang – milieubescherming (voorzieningsbron dicht bij huis), ecologisch beheer, landschapsbehoud, voedselvoorziening, kwaliteitseisen – *daadwerkelijk* ook in het denken van de melkveehouders over zichzelf vooropstaat, hoe meer ruimte het mededingingsrecht biedt voor de regeling. De Commissie heeft langdurige ervaring met het mededingingsrecht en prikt snel en gemakkelijk door een laagje vernis heen dat om een prijsafspraak is gebouwd.

Het is daarbij van belang dat de melkveehouders eveneens onderbouwen waarom deze regeling noodzakelijk is *naast* de al bestaande regelingen van landbouwbeleid: waar schieten deze maatregelen tekort?

5.4 Lobby voor een opgedragen taak van algemeen economisch belang

Hiervoor is uiteengezet dat de melkveehouders wellicht – met de nadruk op *wellicht* – een beroep zouden kunnen doen op de uitzondering, neergelegd in artikel 106 lid 2 VWEU, voor ondernemingen die belast zijn met een dienst van algemeen economisch belang. Maar dat kan alleen, indien de nationale overheid – het ministerie van Economische Zaken en Landbouw ligt hier voor de hand – zich in een regeling, een ministerieel besluit of op andere ondubbelzinnige wijze zou uitspreken over de taak die de melkveehouderij als geheel draagt in het (bijvoorbeeld, en opnieuw) landschapsbehoud, ecologisch beheer, voorziening van basisvoedsel, etc.

Het Verdrag van Lissabon voorziet daarnaast in een mogelijkheid voor de Europese wetgever om op basis van artikel 14 VWEU een regeling op te stellen voor diensten van algemeen economisch belang, waarin de melkveehouderij ook kan worden opgenomen.

Het is echter niet waarschijnlijk dat een dergelijke nationale of Europese regeling op korte termijn wordt gerealiseerd. Bovendien is zelfs als een minister zich in deze zin uitspreekt, daarmee de speelruimte voor de melkveehouders niet onbeperkt: de mededingingsregels blijven gelden, tenzij de toepassing daarvan de opgelegde taak verhindert.

6 Conclusie

De conclusie van de auteurs is dat de Europese regels de melkveehouders weliswaar mogelijkheden geven om tot zelfregulering over te gaan, maar die zijn vooralsnog beperkt. De EU-mededingingsregels – en eventueel nationale mededingingswetgeving – vormen in de eerste plaats het toetsingskader voor initiatieven tot zelfregulering, tenzij de uitzondering van artikel 2 van Verordening 1184/2006 van toepassing is. Maar deze uitzondering wordt door het Hof van Justitie EU en de Europese Commissie eng uitgelegd.

Gezien de mededingingsregels is het van belang de zelfregulering zo vorm te geven dat er geen hardcorerestricties worden opgelegd. Afspraken over prijs en productie zijn in beginsel uit den boze, tenzij de prijs, bijvoorbeeld, slechts een geringe component vormt van de verdere afspraken tussen de melkveehouders. Tegelijkertijd laat de ontwikkeling van het mededingingsrecht zien dat er steeds meer ruimte bestaat om rekening te houden met de specifieke kenmerken van een sector, zoals wellicht de landbouwsector, en publieke belangen, zoals milieubescherming, natuurbehoud en plattelandsontwikkeling. Het Verdrag van Lissabon versterkt de sociale (en publieke) dimensie van de interne markt, waarbij nog meer dan voorheen bij de toepassing van de mededingingsregels rekening gehouden moet worden met 'niet-economische belangen'.

Om er zeker van te zijn dat initiatieven tot zelfregulering niet uiteindelijk afstuiten op de toepassing van de mededingingsregels, is beïnvloeding van politici en mededingingsautoriteiten op Europees (en nationaal) niveau essentieel. Op verschillende fronten kunnen de melkveehouders actie ondernemen en strategieën ontwikkelen ter ondersteuning van hun plannen om over te gaan tot zelfregulering. De instelling van een 'Groep op hoog niveau' laat zien dat de Raad hiervoor niet ongevoelig is. De Commissie wordt derhalve op basis van de uitkomsten van het onderzoek van deze 'Groep op hoog niveau' verzocht om met wetgevingsinitiatieven te komen. Europese regelgeving kan dan het juridisch kader vormen waarbinnen ruimte is voor meer afspraken tussen melkveehouders en melkverwerkers en waarbij de toepassing van de mededingingsregels op de melksector gemitigeerd wordt.

Literatuurlijst

Ambtenbrink & Van de Gronden 2008
F. Amtenbrink en J. van de Gronden, 'Economisch Recht en het Verdrag van Lissabon I – mededinging en interne markt', *SEW*, 2008, p. 325.

Bork 2008
R.H. Bork, *The Antitrust Paradox: A Policy at War with Itself*, Basic Books, 1978.

Gerbrandy 2010
A. Gerbrandy, 'Case Note Case C-8/08, T-Mobile Netherlands BV, KPN Mobile NV, Orange Nederland NV, Vodafone, Libertel NV v. Raad van Bestuur van de Nederlandse Mededingingsautoriteit, Judgement of the Court (Third Chamber) of 4 June 2009, *CML Rev.*, 2010-47, p. 1199-1220.

Gerbrandy 2010
A. Gerbrandy,'Consten en Grundig', in: *Het Recht van de Europese Unie in 50 klassieke arresten,* Den Haag: Boom Juridische Uitgevers 2010, p. 29-37.

Van de Gronden & Mortelmans 2001
J.W. van de Gronden en K.J.M. Mortelmans, *Mededinging en niet-economische belangen*, Deventer: Kluwer 2001.

Houdijk 2009
J. Houdijk, *Publieke belangen in het mededingingsrecht: een onderzoek in vijf domeinen*, Deventer: Kluwer 2009.

Jones & Sufrin 2008
A. Jones & B. Sufrin, *EC Competition Law*, Oxford: Oxford University Press, 2008, p. 28-30.

Kapteyn & VerLoren van Themaat 2003
P. Kapteyn & P. VerLoren van Themaat, *Het recht van de Europese Unie en van de Europese Gemeenschappen*, Deventer: Kluwer 2003.

Marsh & Swanney 1980
J.S. Marsh & P.J. Swanney, *Agriculture and the European Community*, Londen: Allen and Unwin 1980.

McMahon 2007
J.A. McMahon, *EU Agricultural Law*, New York: Oxford University Press 2007.

Monti 2002
G. Monti, 'Article 81 EC and public policy', *Common Market Law Review* 2002.

Townley 2009
C. Townley, *Article 81 EC and public policy*, Oxford and Portland: Hart Publishing 2009.

Vedder 2003
H. Vedder, *Competition Law and Environmental Protection in Europa; Towards Sustainability?*, Groningen: Europa Law Publishing 2003.

Vogelaar 1994
F.O.W. Vogelaar, 'Towards an Improved Integration of EC Environmental Policy and EC Competition Policy: An Interim Report', in: B.E. Hawk (Ed.), *Annual Proceedings of the Fordham Corporate Law Institute – International Antitrust Law & Policy* 1994, The Hague: Kluwer Law International 1995.

De Vries 2006
S.A. de Vries, *Tensions within the Internal Market – The Functioning of the Internal Market and The Development of Horizontal and Flanking Policies*, Groningen: Europa Law Publishing 2006.

Whish 2001
R. Whish, *Competition Law*, London: Butterworths 2001.

Trefwoordenregister

Jurisprudentieregister

Wetsartikelenregister